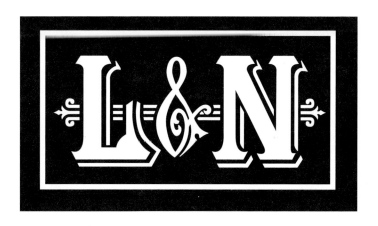

Louisville & Nashville Railroad

The Old Reliable

by
Charles B. Castner
Ronald Flanary
Patrick Dorin

1996
TLC Publishing Inc.
Route 4, Box 154
Lynchburg, VA 24503-9711

Front Cover Illustration:
In his painting, Co-author Ron Flanary has depicted L&N's well-known (if hard to reach) intersection at the mile-long Hagans Tunnel in southwest Virginia, unusual not only for its length but also for the switchback trains from 1930 on were required to negotiate. The intersection also depicts motive power transition, in the shape of L&N's finest in steam, the M-1 2-8-4, and its successor, the Alco FA-2 freight diesels.

Front Endsheet Revered in song and legend, L&N's famed passenger train, *The Pan-American,* headed for Nashville in 1952 behind blue and cream EMD E-units. The train passed South Louisville as switchers worked south end of yard. *C. Norman Beasley/L&N Collection, U Of L Archives*

Back Endsheet: Northbound fast freight train descended Muldraugh Hill on L&N's main line between Elizabethtown and Lebanon Junction, Ky., in summer 1965. Muldraugh was ruling grade for southward trains; old pre-1920s bridge abutment was visible over tops of last two boxcars. *Wm. C. Tayse/L&N Collection, U Of L Archives*

© Copyright 1996
TLC Publishing Inc.

Library of Congress Catalogue Card Number 95-62403
ISBN 1-883089-19-0

Layout and Design by Kenneth L. Miller
Miller Design & Photography, Salem, Va.

Printed by
Walsworth Publishing Co.
Marceline, Mo. 64658

Table of Contents

Patrick C. Dorin came by his interest in railroads at an early age. While still at Northland College in Ashland, Wisconsin., he worked for the Great Northern. Later, he was employed by the Elgin, Joliet & Eastern and the Milwaukee Road. Pat holds degrees in elementary education, school administration and curriculum, also a doctoral degree from the University of Minnesota. He has been an elementary school principal and community education coordinator for the Superior, Wisconsin, public schools and has taught business and education courses parttime at the University of Minnesota-Duluth.

Railroads have continued to hold a strong fascination for Pat, and he has published over 15 pictorial histories of various lines as well as several miscellaneous books on rail subjects. He lives in Superior, WISCONSIN., with his wife Karen.

Ronald C. Flanary has been a life-long admirer of the L&N.

Born in Benham, Kentucky, in 1948 (on L&N's Cumberland Valley Division), Ron was old enough to remember steam's last years on Old Reliable.

After graduation from Clinch Valley College, Ron briefly worked as a management trainee for the Southern Railway. Since 1975, he has been with the LENOWISCO Planning District Commission in Duffield, Virginia, and became its executive director in 1991.

Ron co-authored *L&N in the Appalachians* with Dave Oroszi and Garland McKee, and his many articles and photographs have appeared in *CTC Board, Railfan & Railroad,* and *TRAINS*; he has also done commissioned art work, including a series of paintings for L&N's Safety Department in 1978. Ron's a charter member of the L&N Historical Society and (as of 1995) is its Vice President and Editor of Publications. He and his wife Wilma reside in Big Stone Gap, Virginia.

Charles B. Castner, Jr. retired in 1988 after a long and full career with CSX Transportation and the former L&N. During much of his 27-year rail career, Charlie helped edit the *L&N Magazine* and *Family Lines* as well as handle Public Relations and community relations assignments; he also traveled extensively over the CSXT and L&N systems to gather stories, accompany news media and special groups.

Since retirement, Charlie has served as a volunteer consultant at the University of Louisville Archives, assisting Archives staff in organizing a large collection of L&N-related records. His articles and historical entries have appeared in *TRAINS, Railroad Magazine,* the *Kentucky Encyclopedia of History* and other books and periodicals, and his new book on the NC&StL was published in 1995.

Charlie has been president of the L&N Historical Society since 1991. He and Katie Castner live in Louisville, Kentucky.

Dedication

This book is dedicated to the memory of William H. Kendall, who served as president of the Louisville & Nashville Railroad from 1959 until 1972, and to all former employees and officers, living and deceased, of the company.

Acknowledgements:

The authors wish to thank the following people for sharing their artifacts, memories and time, without which this book would not have been possible:

Karen M. Dorin; Katie Castner, Don Dover of *Extra 2200 South* Magazine, Ralph Gunter, Steve Johnson, Sue Martin of Amtrak, and Frank Schnick.

These persons provided a wide variety of photography from their own cameras or collections: R. D. Acton, Sr.; Frank E. Ardrey; the late Bob Bell, Jr.; James G. Bogle; Wm. N. Clark; Al Chione; Joseph G. Collias, Thomas A. Dorin; Charles Felstead; Dr. R. A. Fontaine; J. B. Fravert; J. Parker Lamb; Bob Lorenz; Shelby Lowe; the late Jerry Mart; Brad McClelland; Garland McKee; David and Jill Oroszi; Howard S. Patrick; Steve Patterson; R. E. Prince; Howard L. Robins; David W. Salter; Harold K. Vollrath and Everett Young.

These former L&N officers and employees reviewed portions of the manuscript: Ira L. Bell, R. Lyle Key; J. G. Lachaussee; P. M. Lanier; J. C. Oaks and Edison H. Thomas.

The authors also wish to thank the University of Louisville Archives for permission to use photographs from the L&N Collection, including many images by the following former L&N public relations staff members: C. Norman Beasley, Donald E. McGregor, William R. Heffren, Robert Kirkpatrick, the late Martin J. Robards; William C. Tayse and Edison H. Thomas

The authors regret any omission of names of other contributors but express again their sincere thanks to all who assisted in one way or another in the writing and production of this book.

Finally, co-authors Castner and Flanary wish to thank Patrick Dorin for his willingness in permitting them to expand his original concept and manuscript in the creation of this book.

Louisville, Ky.
June 25, 1996

L&N Collection, University Of Louisville Archives
L&N bought first road diesels in 1940s, and successful tests against steam led to system dieselization, which began in early 1950s. New Alco FA-2s led empty hoppers back to coal fields in 1954.

Introduction

The late David P. Morgan, editor-emeritus of TRAINS, once wrote that, in his opinion, the L&N was perhaps the least known among major American railroads. However, publication of three books about the railroad and its history may have filled partly the void Morgan felt then existed, at least in the medium of the printed word.

Louisville & Nashville, 1850—1950, the first hard cover book to address the road's historical development, was authored by Kincaid A. Herr, the longtime associate editor of the L&N Magazine.

Book chapters initially appeared as serialized articles in that publication, beginning in the late 1930s. Subsequent editions of Herr's book (which the company itself published) followed in 1950, 1959 and 1964. In 1959, meanwhile, Richard E. Prince, a former member of the mechanical department, wrote and published *Louisville & Nashville Steam Locomotives*, a well illustrated, thorough examination of the road's motive power; Prince produced a revised edition of his locomotive book in 1968, also writing companion books on the NC&StL, Atlantic Coast Line and Seaboard Air Line.

A third book, *History of the Louisville & Nashville Railroad*, appeared in 1972, part of a series of railroad histories from the MacMillan publishing house. Its author was Maury Klein, author and transportation scholar, who in surveying L&N's history, focused most specifically on the road's management leadership and the strategies its top officers devised. Over the years, of course, other books have mentioned the L&N in one way or another to address certain periods of its development, but in the estimation of these authors, the just-mentioned trio of texts provided the definitive coverage of the road and its history. Alas, all have been out of print for some time, and only extant copies remain in private collections or are available at archives, libraries or other repositories.

In no way can *L&N: The Old Reliable* replace what Messrs. Herr, Klein and Prince, respectively, achieved. Rather, it is hoped that this book will complement those and related references and texts by bringing the L&N story forward to its conclusion with the Seaboard System and CSX mergers in the 1980s. Mindful that the Herr, Klein and Prince books were out of print, these authors have included historical sketches of the L&N and its several affiliates, NC&StL, C&EI, Tennessee Central and Monon. Developmental perspectives were also considered, with the several chapters on freight and passenger services, rolling stock and motive power.

Although the L&N is now part of CSX Transportation, it will live on in the hearts of folk from coast to coast and overseas.

Surely it will also be the subject of more investigation and study by historians, students, friends and other researchers in the future. The L&N grew to become a major segment of the American rail transport network. The high quality of service provided by the L&N and its contribution to the region through which it ran made it truly deserving of the title "The Old Reliable!"

L&N Collection, University Of Louisville Archives

Locomotives used by the U.S. Military Railroads occupy trackage in front of the Nashville & Chattanooga's passenger station in Nashville in 1864. During much of war, city served as a major transport hub for the Union advance. The Tennessee state capitol can be seen high on the hill beyond.

A Railroad Is Born

The Louisville and Nashville Railroad came into being on March 5, 1850, when it was granted a charter by the Commonwealth of Kentucky " ...to build a line of railroad between Louisville and the Tennessee state line in the direction of Nashville."

On December 4, 1851, the Tennessee General Assembly authorized the new company to extend its tracks from the Tennessee line south to Nashville. That activity had been preceded by years of interest and agitation, the latter in the form of mass meetings in Bowling Green, Glasgow, Louisville and elsewhere in 1849-50.

Surveyors meanwhile set out in July, 1851 to locate a route, and by summer 1853, crews were at work clearing right of way southward from Louisville. However, the first eight miles of line were not completed until summer, 1855. By then, L&N's founding fathers, most of them Louisville businessmen, had raised $3 million to finance the construction.

On August 25th, the first train steamed south over some eight miles and back of completed track to unofficially celebrate progress to date. Aboard the cars were some 300 passengers including L&N's second president, John Helm. Moving at a then dizzy speed of 15 mph, the special took 27 minutes to make the southward leg, which included three stops, one for water and two to nudge stray cows off the track! The return trip was accomplished in just 20 minutes.

Despite the enthusiasm of promoters and new management, progress was slow, made more difficult by the stubborn terrain enroute, with Muldraugh Hill and Tennessee Ridge to be tunneled through and the Green and Cumberland Rivers to be spanned.

Nonetheless, work proceeded; in mid-June 1858, trackage was completed up Muldraugh, allowing the first train to reach Elizabethtown, 42 miles south of Louisville. By year's end, rails extended beyond Upton, another 20 miles south.

In his fine little book on L&N's first decade, Dr. Thomas D. Clark observed that the construction of the L&N was the largest single internal improvement project undertaken in Kentucky to that time. Completion of the Green River bridge, near Munfordville, by July 1859, removed another major barrier from the path of L&N's builders. The Green was spanned by an iron structure with a total length of 1,800 feet, making it the largest iron bridge then standing in America. By Autumn, Bowling Green in southern Kentucky was reached, and Tennessee Ridge had been pierced

By Train To Nashville

On October 27th, 1859, a flag-bedecked special packed with distinguished citizens and company officers rolled south from Louisville all the way to Nashville to officially open the line.

After a day of revelry in the Tennessee capital city, the train and its passengers returned to Kentucky. Regular train operation commenced on October 31, 1859, making the L&N an accomplished fact.

By then, total investment to complete and equip the road for operation had swollen to $7 million. Excepting war, fire and some lesser interruptions such as floods, trains since have run continuously, between the namesake cities.

At the outbreak of the Civil War, in April 1861, the L&N operated 269 miles of line, including its main stem to Nashville and branches to Bardstown, Lebanon and Guthrie, all in Kentucky.

L&N Collection, University Of Louisville Archives

L&N's commodious new depot at corner of 9th & Broadway, Louisville, opened to the public in 1858. Trainshed behind head house spanned three platforms and six tracks.

At Guthrie, connection was made with the just completed Memphis, Clarksville & Louisville, which with the Memphis & Ohio and L&N, formed a through route to Memphis and the Mississippi Valley.

In War's Path

Situated almost squarely between north and south, the L&N at various times during the Civil War served both the Confederacy and the Union. In the first year of war, the Confederates utilized the L&N to funnel men and supplies into the south, but as battle fronts shifted to Tennessee, Georgia and Alabama, the road became a vital artery for advancing Union forces. Its "wartime chief executive" was James Guthrie, and chief engineer was Albert Fink. Their leadership enabled the L&N to remain in private hands and to operate as efficiently as it did, meeting demands of the public and the U.S. Government.

Time and time again during the war, Confederate forces under General John Hunt Morgan struck at L&N bridges, stations, track and tunnels at points in Kentucky and Tennessee, targeting those facilities for destruc-

tion. However, they didn't reckon with the skill and will of L&N's redoubtable Albert Fink who, after each raid, deployed track crews to repair the damage and restore train service. As the Union offensive rolled southward, the L&N and its connections formed a vital supply route, channeling the necessities of war to advancing Blue armies.

Although it suffered considerable wartime damage, the L&N at the close of hostilities in 1865 found itself in surprisingly good financial condition, so much so that it was able to undertake significant expansion during the next 30 years. Such growth, which resulted from acquisition of other railroads as well as outright construction, extended L&N routes to Cincinnati, Memphis, Birmingham, St. Louis, Evansville and the Gulf Coast port cities of Pensacola, Mobile and New Orleans.

L&N Collection, University Of Louisville Archives

Kentuckian James Guthrie was L&N's president from 1860 to 1868, led road through turbulent Civil War years.

Old building at Mill Street in downtown Lexington, KY., housed first depot for Lexington & Ohio, oldest of L&N's antecedents.

Reconstruction and Expansion

During the late 1860s, L&N assisted the two so-called "Memphis Line" roads - the Memphis, Clarksville & Louisville and the Memphis & Ohio - in restoring trackage and service, and in 1869, the two companies officially came into the fold, being acquired by the larger road that year. Their purchase made possible direct, L&N-single-line train service between Louisville, Bowling Green and Memphis. L&N's Lebanon Branch, meanwhile, was pushed toward the southeast and to an eventual link with Knoxville as well as penetration of the Jellico and Southeastern Kentucky coal fields, the latter via another branch from Corbin. Meanwhile, the Louisville, Cincinnati & Lexington, a connecting road, completed its "Short Line" to Covington, Ky., just south of Cincinnati in 1869 and improved through service to Lexington

(the LC&L was to formally enter the "family" in 1881). A year later, L&N helped open the first bridge across the Ohio at Louisville, to afford a valuable connection to the north and midwest.

By 1872, the L&N had obtained sufficient trackage in Tennessee and Alabama to establish through train service all the way from the Ohio Valley to Montgomery. That step was accomplished by first leasing two railroads, the Nashville & Decatur (which had joined its namesake cities before the Civil War) and South & North Alabama, under construction between Decatur and Montgomery. L&N took over S&NA's construction, completing the route in its entirety in September, 1872.

Birmingham, long referred to as the "Pittsburgh of the South," came into being, largely as a result of the above acquisitions. Over the decades, L&N played a prominent role in Birmingham's growth. Vast deposits of iron and coal lay in the North Alabama region surrounding Birmingham, and the first commercial steel produced there (in 1899) was financed in part by the L&N, which also built a network of lines to tap the rich coal and ore deposits and to serve the region's industries.

Reaching Gulf and World Markets

The L&N's entrance into the Gulf Coast ports of Mobile, New Orleans and Pensacola came in 1880. A 140-mile rail line, the New Orleans & Mobile (completed in 1870), already linked those two namesake cities. Another regional carrier, the Mobile & Montgomery, joined the Alabama port city with the Alabama capital 180 miles to the north, by means of two line segments which had been finished during the years 1861-72. A connection at what today is Flomaton, Al., provided service on to Pensacola.

Acquisition of both the Montgomery and New Orleans roads in 1880-1 gave the L&N a direct Ohio Valley- Gulf Route to those port cities as well as to Biloxi, Gulfport, Pascagoula, and Pensacola. The expansion enabled L&N to extend its sphere of influence to international as well as domestic markets for agricultural and mineral products along with goods produced in on-line cities and regions.

The route from Mobile to New Orleans followed the Gulf Coast (as it does today), and much of the roadbed between the two cities was supported by fills and pilings. Roughly nine miles of trestles and bridges also carried tracks across bays, bayous, inlets, marshes and other waterways. Within a few years of completion of their road, NO&M bridge engineers discovered that the *Teredo Navalis*, a seagoing cousin of the termite, had devoured much of the untreated timbers of those same bridge structures. After considerable investigation, the engineers came up with a treatment process which forced creosote oils under high pressures into the timber. So successful was the process in checking the Teredo, the L&N after acquisition of the NO&M adopted the process and extended such treatment to all bridges and crossties. For many

Louisville, Cincinnati & Lexington (LC&L) built its "Short Line" between LaGrange and Covington, Ky., in 1867-9. Completion of several tall trestles, including one near Independence, marked road's progress through hilly Northern Kentucky. Line became L&N's main stem to Cincinnati in 1881.

years, the railroad also operated a treatment plant near Pascagoula, Ms., to prepare timber poles and other members being installed in coastal bridges and trestles.

During 1879-1881, through purchase of other rail lines in Indiana, Illinois and Kentucky, the L&N gained access to Evansville, St. Louis and the Western Kentucky coal fields. The previously mentioned Short Line (LC&L) was acquired, to officially bring the L&N into the important Cincinnati gateway and also to Lexington, Ky. Elsewhere in the state, work continued in 1881-2 extending the Lebanon Branch through Southeast Kentucky into East Tennessee for a connection to Knoxville, via Jellico, Tn., and a predecessor of the Southern Railway. Through Louisville-Knoxville train service commenced in 1883.

To the South, the L&N-owned Pensacola & Atlantic between 1881-3 pushed rails eastward from that port city across the forested West Florida wilderness some 160 miles to a junction with another railroad which had built west from Jacksonville and Tallahassee. Through train service between Pensacola and Jacksonville began in late 1883, and opening of the P&A (which formally joined L&N in 1895) did much to stimulate growth across the Florida "Panhandle."

In 1891, the Kentucky Central's Covington-Winchester-Livingston route was purchased, and early penetration of the Southeastern Kentucky coal fields was accomplished, with the opening of a line to Norton, Va., via Pineville and Middlesborough, Ky. In all, more than 50 smaller railroads were acquired, leased or built by the L&N during the 1880s and 1890s, as the L&N system began to take final form. It was also in the early 1880s that the now familiar red "L&N" emblem first appeared on stationery and promotional materials, the emblem having been designed by the Louisville Shops' master painter, George Schumpp. The enduring nickname "Old Reliable" originated from that time as well.

Improvements on Many Fronts

Technical progress also kept pace with L&N's geographic expansion. Steel replaced iron in rails, and track width was standardized from several varying gauges to one common gauge- 4 feet 9 inches—so that L&N passenger and freight cars could be interchanged with cars of

L&N Collection, University Of Louisville Archives

Pensacola also provided the L&N with a Gulf port, the railroad obtaining trackage to the city in 1880, then during the next two decades building extensive facilities for export and import traffic.

A 4-4-0 of Taunton Locomotive Works(1864) ancestry headed mixed train on Greensburg, Ky., branch near Campbellsville in the 1880s. Part of rival Nashville-Cincinnati route never finished, branch came into L&N fold in 1879, was abandoned a century later.

One of L&N's oldest locomotives, No. 20, *Quigley* was assembled by Moore & Richardson in Cincinnati in 1859, was confiscated by Confederates during Civil War. Engine was pictured at Louisville after war's end.

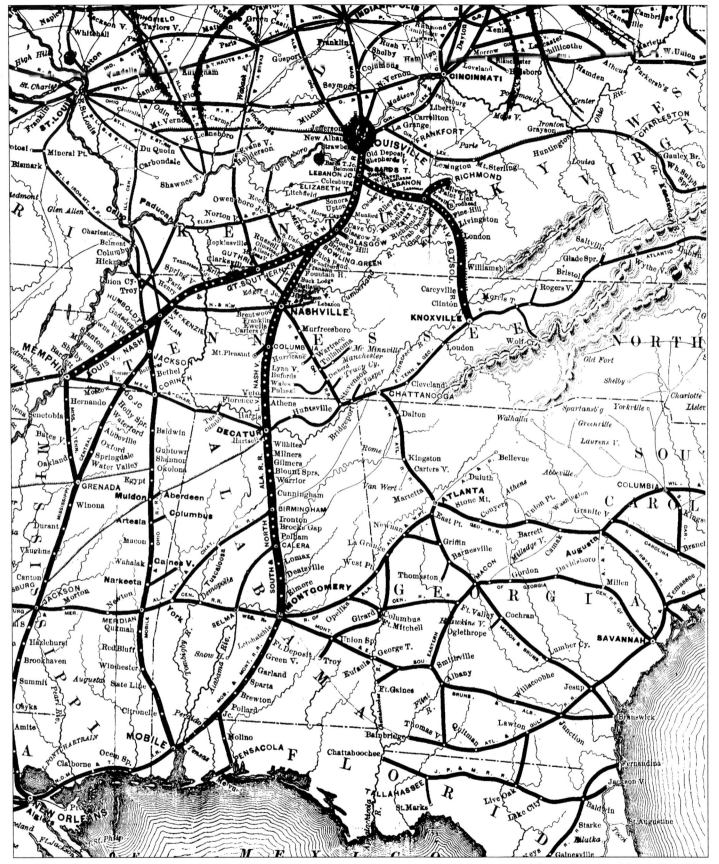

Map from 1875 timetable showed L&N's southward development after Civil War. Road had just completed the South & North Alabama's main trunk in September 1872, offering through train service between Ohio Valley, Birmingham and Montgomery. Memphis Line was in full operation, and Knoxville Branch, opened to Livington, Ky., pointed toward that city-goal.

During the last weekend in May 1886, L&N forces changed some 3,000 miles of track from five feet to four feet, nine inches. At the same time, shops forces reduced the width of hundreds of car and locomotive axles for the new gauge. The event was depicted by an L&N Magazine cover from 1940.

other railroads. During the last weekend in May, 1886, L&N forces changed some 2,000 miles of track from the five-foot gauge to standard. Wheels of hundreds of locomotives and cars likewise were shifted so that they could operate on the new track gauge.

Larger and heavier steam locomotives with more driving wheels replaced the diminutive "tea kettles" of earlier years, and coal replaced wood as fuel for motive power. The adoption of the air brake and the automatic coupler, along

with electric signals, switches and improved communications greatly improved the safety of railroad operations. Wooden passenger cars began to give way to all-steel cars with enclosed vestibules, and freight cars began a similar transition, from wood to steel construction. Special types of freight cars were introduced to handle the diverse list of commodities being produced by on-line industries.

The person most closely identified with L&N's emergence as a major rail carrier was Milton H. Smith, who was its president for 33 years, or between 1884-1886 and 1891-1921. Wrote Maury Klein in his history of the L&N, "During that long reign, Smith influenced the course of the system's destiny more than any other man in its history except Albert Fink." (Fink was chief engineer in L&N's formative years, later became vice president).

Smith came to work for the L&N as a local freight agent in Louisville, just after the Civil War. Within three years, he had advanced to general freight agent, eventually becoming vice president and traffic manager and, finally, president in 1884. Controversial yet purposeful, Smith shaped the L&N from a small regional carrier into one of America's major railroad systems. Klein adds, "...It was Smith who did much to rationalize L&N's administration into a cohesive structure capable of dealing with the complex problems of the inter-territorial era...and who devised and promulgated a viable developmental strategy for that era."

Controversial yet purposeful, Milton H. Smith led L&N for 33 years, or from the 1880s until his death in 1921.

German-born, Albert Fink came to L&N in 1857 as its chief engineer, kept the road repaired and operating during the Civil War. He later became general superintendent and vice president.

A New Century And Into Coal Country

The L&N was 50 years old in 1900 but was still growing. Between 1902-7, a new "second main line" was completed through Eastern Tennessee and North Georgia, linking Cincinnati, Knoxville and Atlanta. Soon after, important feeder branches diverging from that route were acquired or built to penetrate the vast coal fields of Eastern and Southeastern Kentucky, also East Tennessee. That work became one of the L&N's most important expansions, and to support such growth, a huge system shop for cars and locomotives was opened in 1905 at Louisville. Management and other administrative employees based in the city also moved into a new general office building in 1907.

Acquisition in 1909-10 of the former Lexington & Eastern and Louisville & Atlantic Railroads brought L&N to the rich bituminous fields surrounding Breathitt, Letcher and Perry Counties in Kentucky, and construction of new trackage along the North Fork of the Kentucky River in 1911-12 extended rails from Hazard to Whitesburg and Fleming in the far eastern corner of the state. A year later, the first loaded hoppers began rolling from Hazard-area mines to national markets.

Concurrently with Eastern Kentucky developments, the L&N constructed new branches from its Cumberland Valley Branch to serve mines being developed in Bell and Harlan Counties, Kentucky, with coal moving from Harlan, beginning in August 1912. In succeeding decades, the L&N built additional lines, not only in Eastern and Southeastern Kentucky but also in the Commonwealth's Western fields as well as in Southern Indiana and Illinois, and Alabama and Tennessee. Segments of the Cincinnati, Cumberland Valley and Eastern Kentucky Divisions were given two tracks to better handle the flood-tide of coal rolling from mines to markets; terminals and yards were also expanded at Corbin, Covington, Harlan, Hazard and Ravenna, in Kentucky, and Etowah, in Tennessee.

World War I curtailed much of L&N's program of additions, betterments and expansion. Great demands were placed on all railroads to move troops and materiel in support of the war effort, and the L&N itself transported thousands of men to training camps across the south. So severe did the shortage of rolling stock become, all railroads, including the L&N, were taken over and operated by the Federal Government from 1917 until 1920.

Eastern Kentucky Mountain folk swarmed about L&N ten-wheeler 324 as she brought the first work train into Hazard in June 1912. Few had seen a train before.

Chaska Tenn

Construction forces finished new water tank and station at Chaska, Tenn., on L&N's "second main line" near the Kentucky state line about 1904-5.

B&B forces erected a new double-track bridge at Emerling, Ky., in May 1926 on L&N's Cumberland Valley Division as part of extensive system double-tracking and upgrading accomplished during the decade.

Prosperity and New Trains

By contrast, the 1920s brought real prosperity to the nation and to L&N Land. The railroad initiated many improvements. new rolling stock and heavier, more powerful locomotives were purchased; segments of main lines were double-tracked for increased post-war traffic; automatic block signals and stronger bridges (for heavier motive power) were installed on many of the Old Reliable's divisions. Also in the decade, L&N began publishing its company employee magazine and offering group insurance, service buttons and passes to employees.

The prosperous 1920s also introduced new trains, such as the *Pan-American* on the Cincinnati-New Orleans mainline, the *Crescent Limited* on the Gulf Coast segment of its Washington-New Orleans run, and fine new seasonal trains for the popular Midwest-Florida travel trade. In 1929, the road also acquired the Louisville, Henderson & St. Louis Railway, giving it a direct Ohio Valley-St. Louis gateway route. And, in 1930, completion of the mile-long Hagans Tunnel in southwest Virginia provided the L&N with a much needed "eastern" connection for its Cumberland Valley Division. The new

L&N Collection, University Of Louisville Archives

New train for a new decade, *The Pan-American* rolled into Louisville on December 5, 1921, on its inaugural run from Cincinnati to New Orleans. Famed train later went all-Pullman, also became a "radio star" during the 1930s.

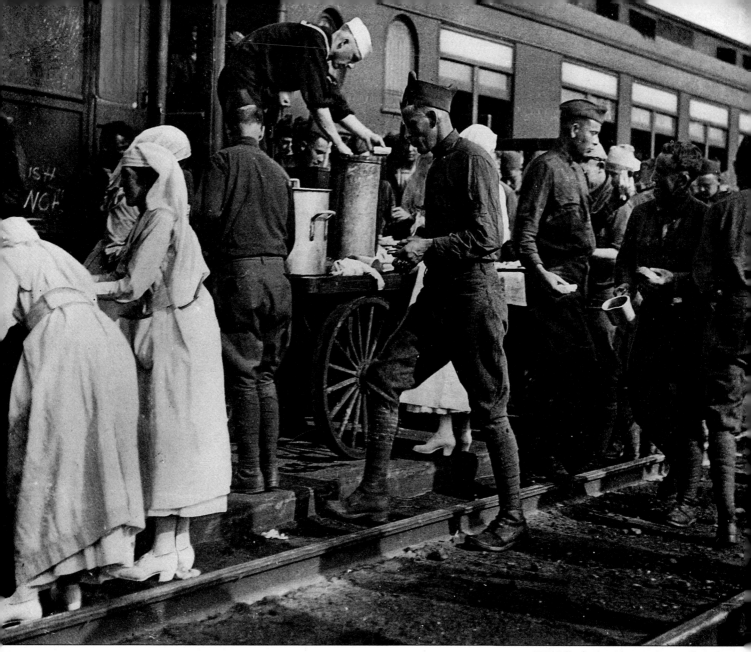

L&N Collection, University Of Louisville Archives

Sailors and soldiers helped Red Cross volunteers distribute food aboard an L&N troop train at Union Station, Louisville, during World War One.

tunnel and related trackage linked the CV with the "family owned" Clinchfield so that coal could move more directly from Southeastern Kentucky to markets in the Carolinas.

The Depression-dominated 1930s meant an overall "tightening of the belt" for the L&N, and to keep its "head above water," so to speak, the company was forced to reduce wages, furlough many employees and curtail train services on marginal routes. Over 200 miles of branch lines were also abandoned during the decade. The January 1937 Ohio Valley flood, in truth, did submerge portions of routes on L&N's north

end to disrupt operations for two weeks.

Nonetheless, during the 30s, L&N achieved progress on several fronts. Air conditioning was introduced on all principal passenger trains; pick-up-and-delivery service of LCL or less-than-carload freight shipments was inaugurated, and schedules of several freight trains were speeded up to provide shippers expedited overnight service between major cities on the system. And, as forerunners of a major shift in rail motive power, two diesel-electric switch engines joined L&N's locomotive fleet in fall 1939.

The great Ohio Valley flood of January 1937 inundated much of L&N's "north end," including the Cincinnati, Evansville and Louisville Terminals as well as some 200 miles of line. Ohio River waters swirled through Union Station, Louisville; the general office building, cold and vacant, stood to the rear.

World War Two and Toward a New Century

The L&N and other American railroads were called upon to move unprecedented numbers of passengers and record volumes of freight during World War II (1941-45). More than 90 per cent of all military equipment and supplies and 97 per cent of all troops rolled by rail to military bases and ports of embarkation. Fed by dozens of on-line training camps and defense plants, L&N's own traffic loads soared, with increases of 80 percent in freight and over 300 percent in passengers. And yet, the successful handling of that traffic surge was done with comparatively little addition to motive power, rolling stock or personnel. During the War, some 6,900 employ-

Several hundred miles of lightly trafficked branch lines across the system were abandoned during the 1930s and 40s; rails and track materials from some branches went to World War II scrap drives, including this bridge and its spans at Irvine, Ky., on the old L&A (Louisville & Atlantic) Branch.

ees served in the Armed Forces; of that number, 112 gave their lives. The 728th Railway Operating Battalion, many of its officers and enlisted men from L&N ranks, served with distinction in Europe and helped rebuild and operate war-ravaged rail systems there.

The immediate postwar years brought dramatic changes to railroads - most surely to the L&N. The most dramatic, single change, perhaps, came in motive power, as steam locomotives, for a century railroading's prime movers, began to step aside for the more efficient, cleaner diesel-electrics. As previously noted, L&N bought its first diesel units - two switch engines - in late 1939. During World War II, 16 road passenger diesels went into service between Cincinnati, New Orleans and Atlanta, showing just how well the new power could perform.

Then, following the War, hundreds of new passenger, freight and switcher-type diesels were purchased, replacing ranks of travel-weary steamers, many built before 1920.

Other noteworthy improvements came in the postwar years. L&N's first lightweight streamlined passenger trains, the "Humming Bird" and "Georgian," were inaugurated (in November 1946) between Cincinnati and New Orleans

and St. Louis and Atlanta, respectively. CTC or Centralized Traffic Control, which first made its introduction on several busy wartime routes, was extended over hundreds of miles of main and important secondary lines to expedite train movements and, on some routes, permit removal of second main tracks. Thousands of new special purpose freight cars were bought, and hundreds of older cars were modernized at the South Louisville Shops. Greater mechanization of trackwork and other roadway maintenance was undertaken, and additional branch lines were built in Eastern and Western Kentucky to serve newly developed coal mines for post-War business expansion.

March 5, 1950, marked L&N's one hundredth anniversary. At that date, the road operated 4,780 miles of first-main track and about 8,000 miles of all track. Motive power included 640 steam locomotives and 202 diesel units, with 88 more on order. L&N also owned 635 passenger cars and 61,300 freight cars, with orders for another 6,950 cars having been placed. There were 28,000 employees and 15,000 stockholders, the latter residing in all of the-then 48 states.

President James B. Hill addressed thousands of Louisville employees and their families at Family Rally in July 1935. Similar "Friendly Service" rallies were held throughout the system to bring about better understanding between employees and the public they served.

Robert L.Kirkpatrick/L&N Collection, University Of Louisville Archives

L&N transported record volumes of passengers during World War II (1941-45); many service men and women were accommodated in cars of regularly scheduled trains.

Surely "queen" of L&N's big city passenger stations, Union Station at l0th and Broadway, Louisville, was completed in late September 1891. Last used by the railroad in 1976, the Romanesque structure today is headquarters for the city's mass transit company.

Into The Second Century, and Beyond   2

The 1950s were prosperous years for the L&N, thanks in no little part to the postwar expansion of business and industry throughout the South.

Generally strong freight revenues enabled the company to continue major technological improvements started in the previous decade. New electronic freight marshalling yards were built in Nashville, Atlanta and Birmingham to speed up the classification of freight traffic passing through those major cities. Piggyback —or trailer-on-flatcar (TOFC) movements— began on the L&N in 1955, when several test trailer shipments moved from Louisville to Birmingham and New Orleans. Movement of new autos and trucks also commenced then, first as single shipments of over-the-road trailers, also piggyback style, but later in specially developed multi-level rack cars. Both services were to grow mightily in the 1960s and 70s (See Chapter 7).

CTC installations on main and secondary routes continued through the decade; more new streamlined coaches and sleeping cars were added to the consists of leading passenger trains, and new stations were opened in Birmingham, Mobile and New Orleans. Finally, the switch from steam power to diesel was accomplished in 1957, when the last active steamers were withdrawn from service and sent to the scrap heap. To dieselize completely, L&N had spent $87 million for the new locomotives. Actually, costs went even higher, when expenses to upgrade shops and servicing facilities and retrain maintenance and train crews were added in.

Merger With NC&StL

Enlargement of L&N's physical size took place in August 1957, with the merger of the Nashville, Chattanooga & St. Louis Railway into the larger system. The new acquisition added another 1,200 miles to parent L&N and provided direct lines from Nashville to Atlanta and Memphis. The merger, first to occur in modern U.S. rail history, also consummated a long L&N-NC&StL corporate relationship that reached back to 1880.

L&N Collection,
University Of Louisville Archives

L&N called its version of piggyback "TOTE" (for "Trailer On Train Express"). The new freight service was inaugurated in 1955 with test shipments between Louisville and cities in South.

Nashville, Chattanooga & St. Louis Railway

In point of history, the NC&StL was even older than the L&N, the incorporation of its antecedent (and Tennessee's first railroad), the Nashville & Chattanooga, occurring in 1845. Still older was the Western & Atlantic, chartered in 1830 and later to provide the N&C access through North Georgia to Atlanta. By 1854, the N&C had pierced Cumberland Mountain in southeast Tennessee to finish its main trunk into Chattanooga and a connection with the W&A to Atlanta. That through route, together with L&N's main line from Louisville to Tennessee, was to give Union General Sherman a most vital supply route supporting the advance of his armies into Georgia during 1864.

In the post-Civil War decades, the N&C expanded, in 1873 acquiring the former Nashville & Northwestern and its route from the Tennessee capital west to the Mississippi River at Hickman, Ky. To reflect its growth and aspirations, the road also added "St. Louis" to its corporate name, and during the decade, branch line railroads in Tennessee and Alabama were brought into its fold.

E.W. Cole, NC&StL's visionary president, dreamed of an even larger system, attempting to acquire additional trackage in Kentucky, Southern Indiana and Illinois. L&N's reaction to this move into its territory was to purchase a majority of NC&StL stock (in 1880) and take over the lines it had bid for.

Notwithstanding control from Louisville, the NC&StL continued to grow, leasing in 1896 a Paducah-Memphis route formed by the former Paducah, Tennessee & Alabama and Tennessee Midland companies. The route intersected NC&StL at Hollow Rock (later Bruceton), and the Memphis leg, in turn, created a direct link to and from Nashville. From the 1890s on, the NC&StL also served as an important link in a Midwest-Florida route by participating with the L&N, Chicago & Eastern Illinois, and several roads south of Atlanta - notably Atlantic Coast Line - in the flow of much seasonal freight and passenger traffic, including the long remembered *Dixie Flyer* and other *"Dixie"* fleet trains.

The L&N-NC&StL merger in 1957 kicked off a procession of modern day mergers in the rail industry. In the highly competitive transportation market of the post World War II decades, it made sense for the L&N to merge its subsidiary into the larger system. Not only were single-line services created between the two roads on certain routes, but also greater economies in operations and equipment utilization were achieved after the merger.

Even before 1957, NC&StL at Nashville had shifted all freight operations to L&N's larger, more modern Radnor Yard (partially automated and expanded in 1954); in Atlanta, NC&St.L's former Hills Park Yard was modernized and enlarged to include L&N's train movements. A new yard at Wauhatchie, near Chattanooga, in 1961 replaced the older Cravens Yard in the city. The former NC&StL added some 4,000 employees and 1,043 miles of lines in Alabama, Georgia, Kentucky and Tennessee to the L&N system.

L&N Collection, University Of Louisville Archives

NC&StL eight-wheeler No.49 paused with Tracy City Branch passenger train No.121 at Monteagle, Tenn., in 1910. Built by the Sewanee Mining Company before the Civil War, the branch came into NC&StL ownership in 1887, was abandoned by the L&N almost a century later.

Pioneering Nashville & Chattanooga conquered Cumberland Mountain in Tennessee with a 2,200-foot long tunnel in the early 1850s. Successor NC&StL used historic locale for promotional photos, this from 1945, with 4-8-4 on main line(tunnel mouth), 2-8-0 on Tracy City Branch tracks, above.

New President and New Decade

As the 1950s drew to a close, John Tilford, president since 1950, stepped down, to be replaced (in April 1959) by William H. Kendall, then executive vice president. Before coming to the L&N in 1954, Kendall had served as general manager of the Clinchfield Railroad and earlier had held various management supervisory positions with the Atlantic Coast Line and Pennsylvania Railroads. On October 24, 1959, the centennial of completion of the main line (in October 1859) was marked by the running of a special train between Louisville and Nashville. L&N's century-just-ended with steam motive power received a final salute from the run, which was powered by a borrowed steam locomotive from neighboring Illinois Central (L&N by then had retired all of its own steamers).

Steam power, happily, made a brief return in the early 1960s, in the guise of the historic Civil War engine "General," which also became focus of a successful publicity and community relations campaign launched by the L&N. A key participant in the Civil War Andrews Raid episode in Georgia (later popularized as the Great Locomotive Chase), the engine barnstormed some 20,000 miles in 17 states during 1962-5 as part of centennial commemorative events marking the conflict. From the trips and with use of a treasured heirloom (the "General"), L&N also demonstrated a century of technical development in railroading.

New Computers, Cars and Welded Rail

Continued progress throughout the 1960s was evidenced in the introduction of computers and data processing to revolutionize a host

Centralized Traffic Control spread across more divisions in the 1950s-60s. Dispatcher H. D. Harrod worked the big Louisville Division CTC console; two center panels covered main line; Lebanon Branch was at left.

Air and highway travel claimed much of L&N's intercity passenger travel after 1950s, despite lower fares, new equipment and faster schedules offered public.

Wm. C. Tayse/L&N Collection, University Of Louisville Archives

L&N bought first computer system in early 1960s to process routine accounting chores; by the 1970s computers performed host of procedures for many departments.

of administrative and operating procedures in virtually every activity on the L&N. A data processing department, organized in 1962, was greatly expanded into Management Information Services by 1968. That led a year later to creation of Cybernetics & Systems, L&N's first non-rail subsidiary, which developed software as well as managed various data systems within and outside the railroad.

Specialized freight car types continued to be introduced by the L&N to meet specific needs of shippers, and intermodal traffic - piggyback and automotive (autos and trucks) - grew at record levels during the decade. Several all trailer-container and/or auto trains went into service to meet the increase in traffic, especially on routes from Chicago and Cincinnati to Atlanta. Ramps with mechanized equipment to handle trailers were opened at dozens of communities, and modern auto-loading/storage yards went on-line at Louisville, Nashville, Birmingham, Memphis, Atlanta and New Orleans. To transport King Coal from mines to market, L&N also made far greater use of unit train operations (with fast load/unloading facilities at originating and terminating points). Coal continued to account for almost 40 per cent of L&N's total freight tonnage, with a major share moving in unit trains.

C. Norman Beasley/L&N Collection, University Of Louisville Archives

L&N first began installing continuous welded rail (CWR) in its mainline trackage in 1958. Early installations were made on then- Mobile, New Orleans & Pensacola Division that fall.

On the track/roadway front, L&N installed 900 miles of continuously welded rail (CWR) into mainline trackage during the decade, much of that produced by its new Rail Welding facility in Nashville (which opened in 1965). There, 39 foot rail sections were welded into quarter-mile lengths, then moved to field locations for installation. CTC was extended to more lines during the '60s, covering nearly 2,500 main line and secondary route miles by decade's end, and the first links of a microwave system were installed between Louisville and Corbin.

While freight traffic remained strong, in part due to coal and intermodal traffic growth, passenger revenues - and the trains producing them - spiraled downward. Miles of new federally-funded Interstate highways captured more and more intercity travelers during the 1960s, as did commercial jet aviation, and by 1970, the eve of Amtrak, L&N operated just two mainline passenger trains.

Two "tough ladies" - Gulf Coast Storms - took swipes at the L&N during the '60s. Hurricane Betsy struck in September 1965, knocking out 33 miles of main line between Mobile and New Orleans for three weeks and damaging many bridges, signals and commu-

Two Pioneers, Pontchartrain and Lexington & Ohio

By virtue of their antiquity, two small railroads, which later became part of the L&N system, need brief recognition here. These were the Pontchartrain, in the greater New Orleans area, and the Lexington & Ohio, in Central Kentucky. Pontchartrain's trackage ran about 4.5 miles from New Orleans to Milneburg, on the namesake lake; the more ambitious Lexington intended to build west from its terminus city to some point on the Ohio River near Louisville.

Both railroads were chartered within 10 days of each other in January 1830, which closely followed the formation of the Baltimore & Ohio, in 1827; both lines were readied for traffic (albeit with flesh and blood horsepower!) a year or two later - April 14, 1831, for the Pontchartrain, and August 15, 1832, for the first six miles of the Lexington line. Each also laid claim to being the very first railroad west of the Alleghenies.

Pontchartrain managements also envisioned expansion, possibly to Mobile, but such plans never materialized. Instead, the line, opting for steam power over horses by the mid 1830s, contented itself for the next century as mostly a commuter carrier, conveying New Orleans folk from a station in Elysian Fields (later, Pontchartrain Junction, in L&N timetables) to the lake and back. The little road came into the L&N fold in 1880, thereafter borrowed from its parent motive power and cars for its trains, which locals dubbed "Smoky Mary." Last passenger runs were made in March 1932, with total abandonment three years later.

The Lexington & Ohio, meanwhile, pushed its rails on to Frankfort, 29 miles to the west, reaching the second city by 1834. Steam locomotives replaced Old Dobbin a year later, but the nationwide financial panic of 1837 precluded any track being laid west of Frankfort. Later, another railroad, the Louisville & Frankfort (L&F), did complete what the L&O had failed to do, finishing trackage between the two cities by 1851. Still later, the L&F and L&O (the latter having also reorganized) consolidated operations to provide continuous train service from Louisville to Lexington; after the Civil War, the merged road (Louisville, Cincinnati & Lexington, or LC&L) also built the so-called "Short Line" from LaGrange to Covington, Ky., then joined the larger L&N system in 1880. The "Short Line" of course became L&N's Cincy-Louisville mainline, while the Louisville-Lexington route eventually formed the west end of the Eastern Kentucky Division.

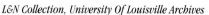

L&N Collection, University Of Louisville Archives

Hurricanes *Betsy* and *Camille* visited L&N Land in 1965/69, disrupting train movements across Gulf for week or more. Chief Engineer J. B. Clark and a Mobile Division engineering officer examine damaged signals near English Lookout, La.

C. Norman Beasley/L&N Collection, University Of Louisville Archives

New passenger stations were opened at Mobile, New Orleans and Birmingham during the 1950s, early 1960s. Mobile station, above, also housed division offices.

nication lines. Four years later, Storm Camille wreaked havoc in the same area. But, company forces toiled around the clock to open trackage 17 days later.

TC, C&EI and Monon "Grow" System

The L&N System grew once again, in the late 1960s-early 1970s, with acquisition of all or parts of three smaller railroads in Tennessee, Illinois and Indiana. In March, 1969, the L&N purchased 135 miles of the former Tennessee Central Railroad (TC) between Nashville and Crossville, Tn.. to serve communities and their industries in the Middle and North Central regions of the state.

Then three months later, in June, L&N acquired the so-called "eastern" line of the former Chicago & Eastern Illinois Railroad (C&EI). The acquisition added 287 route miles to the system, including a main line segment from Woodland Junction, Ill., near Danville, to Evansville, Ind., as well as a branch to Mount Vernon, Ind. It also provided the L&N access to the vast Chicago gateway and market and permitted the railroad to provide shippers with scheduled single-line service from the Great Lakes to the Gulf Coast, Central South and Southeast.

Finally, in August 1971, the L&N purchased the 541-mile Monon Railroad, which offered a second entrance into Chicago by way of Bloomington and Lafayette, In. Branches also served Indianapolis, Michigan City, French Lick and coal fields near Midland, all in Indiana (see sidebars for brief historical sketches of the C&EI, Monon and TC).

The 1960s marked the last full decade L&N was to operate as an independent company under its own management and with its own corporate structure and stockholders. Measured against previous periods of history, L&N's achievements during the decade were impressive. During 1968, total assets for the road passed the one-billion mark for the first time; system mileage stood at some 6,000

New auto and truck traffic returned to L&N, other railroads in a big way, beginning in the 1960s; vehicles were carried on multi-level rack cars.

miles (which grew to 6,500 miles in 1971 after the Monon merger); and revenue ton-miles - tons of customer freight carried one mile (a key yardstick in railroading) - rose to more than 29.1 billion by 1969. Revenue ton miles, which stood at about 12.7 billion in December 1949, increased 130 percent by 1969.

The "Family" Expands

The decade of the 1970s was one of transition and great change for the L&N, corporately as well as operations-wise. The decade also was not without difficulties - and some tragedy. From a corporate perspective, the most significant change came in 1972 with acquisition of all L&N common stock by Seaboard Coast Line Industries (SCLI) of Jacksonville, Fl., which had just been formed and by then held all stock of the Seaboard Coast Line Railroad. SCLI, it might be noted, also followed in the wake of the Atlantic Coast Line-Seaboard (ACL/SAL) rail merger of 1967. Thus, the above activity, as it pertained to the L&N, was not totally unexpected, and in reality had been long anticipated in business and transportation circles.

In fact, L&N's relationship with the former Atlantic Coast Line extended back to the beginning of the century, or to 1902, when Coast Line under leadership of Henry Walters purchased 51 percent

With advent of Family Lines System in 1970s, L&N joined SCL and other member roads to coordinate freight services. A New Orleans-Jacksonville "run-through" crosses the long pre-stressed concrete bridge at Bay St. Louis, Miss.

of L&N's common stock from J. P. Morgan interests. Even older was the lease of the Georgia Railroad, which L&N had acquired in 1898 from the Georgia Railroad & Banking Company, which in turn also leased the West Point Route properties (Atlanta & West Point and Western of Alabama Railways). Early on, traffic patterns developed between these several "family" roads, with considerable volumes of freight and passenger traffic interchanged at Atlanta, Birmingham and Montgomery (with, respectively, Georgia, ACL-affiliate AB&C and Coast Line proper).

Then, in 1924-5, ACL and L&N obtained the lease of the Clinchfield, Carolina & Ohio Ry. (Clinchfield). Built primarily as a coal hauler in the early 1900s, CC&O ran from Elkhorn City, Ky., through Southwest Virginia, East Tennessee and Western North Carolina to a ter-minus in Spartanburg, S.C. L&N's late- 1920s extension of its Cumberland Valley Division (via the 6500-foot long Hagans Tunnel) was intended to form an "eastern" outlet for CV-originated coal as well as provide access to the Clinchfield and markets in the Carolinas (see also Chapter 8 for a more detailed discussion of those activities as well as a description of L&N's coal hauling operations).

The interchange for coal and other traffic L&N established with Clinchfield at Miller Yard, Va. (via Interstate R.R. trackage) was further improved in the 1970s, when L&N obtained track rights from N&W to run from Norton to St. Paul, VA., to directly access CRR's main line. At Spartanburg, CRR's southern terminus, traf-fic flowed to and from ACL's affiliate Charleston & Western Carolina (C&WC). W. H. Kendall served as Clinchfield's manager before

C. Norman Beasley/L&N Collection, University Of Louisville Archives

New machines and techniques helped improve L&N's track maintenance. Behind undercutter, track forces laid new stablization fabric, improving drainage on mainline near Cartersville, Ga., in early 1980.

becoming L&N's president in 1959, and C. S. Sanderson, who followed Mr.Kendall at Erwin, Tn., CRR's operating headquarters,later came to the L&N as vice president-operations.

ACL and its rival SAL, paralleling each other in markets along the East Coast and in Florida, began discussing merger in the early 1960s. However, ACL's ownership of the L&N and opposition by other major railroads in the region delayed the consolidation until 1967. Earlier in the decade, ACL had moved its headquarters from Wilmington, N.C., to Jacksonville, Fl., and at the latter city had built a large new general office building, which later was to become headquarters for SCL Industries as well as base for the developing Family Lines Rail System.

The new "System" embraced SCL, the L&N, Clinchfield, Georgia and the two West Point Route roads, Atlanta & West Point and Western Railway of Alabama. L&N ranked second in size, with SCL being the largest. Together, the five lines made up a 16,000-mile system that reached from Richmond, Norfolk and Charleston on the east coast, Chicago, Cincinnati and St. Louis in the Midwest to Florida, the Gulf Coast and New Orleans. A combined power and rolling stock fleet counted collectively 2,500 locomotives, 10,000 trailers and 141,000 freight cars. The "Family Lines Rail System" name was adopted to market services offered by the five railroads, and common emblem, logo and color schemes were introduced for everything, from letterhead to

"Old and new" in Monon diesels, EMD BL-2 and GE U23B units are spotted side by side at Lafayette, Ind., in 1970.

terminal signs to freight cars and locomotives.

While each "family" road including L&N retained its identity, coordination between the lines proceeded on several fronts, notably in administration, marketing and operations. Across the Southeast and Midwest, sales offices and their staffs were integrated, and several departments from each line came to be consolidated, some at L&N's general office building and others at SCL's Jacksonville headquarters. At the latter city, new fourth generation computers took over compiling car movement data for all five railroads.L&N's Operations Center at Louisville was duplicated at Jacksonville for SCL, while at Atlanta, a new regional "Transportation Center" was created in 1975 in the former Tilford Yard freight house to house L&N, Georgia-West Point and Seaboard train dispatchers and, in L&N's case, its Atlanta Division CTC board. Resident officers for the roads, together with area sales and marketing folk also moved in to the Center.

New Leadership, More Coordination

Overall corporate leadership also changed. Prime F. Osborn, who had been a member of L&N's law department in the 1950s and more recently president of SCL Industries, returned to Louisville in 1972 to head the L&N. W. H. Kendall became vice-chairman of SCLI, while W. Thomas Rice, long ACL's top officer, presided over the SCL in Jacksonville. Later in the decade, Mr. Rice was named chairman of Industries, and Mr. Osborn assumed presidency of both railroads, Seaboard and L&N.

More coordination, operations-wise, also occurred during the 70s, within "the Family." L&N's modern Tilford Yard at Atlanta was further enlarged for SCL trains, as were Boyles Yard in Birmingham and the S&NA Yard in Montgomery. Several runthrough train routes also began, as "Family Roads" took advantage of the shortest routes across the south to give shippers faster, more direct train services.

On L&N proper, the South Louisville Shops were extensively upgraded in 1974-5, and a new automated classification yard for Louisville opened in 1977 to greatly improve terminal operations and train movements in and out of L&N's headquarters city. New Divisional operations centers with upgraded computer-assisted CTC boards also went in at Louisville, Evansville and Corbin, and centrally located Customer Service Centers and their staffs, utilizing the latest in telecommunications to better serve shippers, began replacing individual stations at many localities. On some L&N and SCL divisions, Mobile Agents in specially equipped vans worked from CSCs to reach more rural on-line areas. Unproductive branch lines continued to be pared from the system, while some marginally profitable branches were taken over by regional carriers or other operating entities.

Coal Shifts to Southland

L&N's traditional coal traffic patterns were to also dramatically change in the 1970s. For years, "L&N" coal moved mostly northbound to Midwest and Northeastern markets. But, with the great growth of Southland utilities in the 1960s and early 70s to match that region's industrialization, the demand for coal shifted significantly. For L&N, the shift meant wrestling heavy coal tonnage trains from Corbin and Nashville southward to Atlanta over mostly single track mountainous profiles.

Albeit a blessing in one sense, L&N's increased traffic (in 1973 up 60 percent over the previous decade) took its toll in power, rolling stock, track wear and line congestion. An archaic system which allocated cars to mine tipples for loading began to exacerbate equipment shortages. Traditionally low coal rates also failed to provide L&N the yield it badly needed for more cars, engines, line and terminal improvements. Then in 1979, a 22 per cent rate increase authorized by the Interstate Commerce Commission did finally give the road sufficient capital to acquire new motive power and open top hoppers and commence important roadway and yard improvements on its coal-hauling lines.

Sadly, during the decade, L&N was to experience accidents at Pensacola, Fl.(1977), and Waverly, Tenn. (1978), both involving trains handling hazardous materials in tank cars and both resulting in loss of life. It was the aftermath of the Waverly accident - the explosion of one of the involved tank cars-that took such a human toll—16 city fire fighters and railroad personnel lost their lives. But, from lessons learned at Pensacola and Waverly, the L&N and other railroads upgraded response procedures for all hazardous cargo emergencies. They also helped develop new train-handling techniques and assisted the chemical and shipping industries in improving tank car designs with protective gear.

Richard D. Spence was L&N's president from 1978-81 and oversaw many of the improvements noted in the above paragraphs. With years of operating experience on the Southern Pacific and most recently Conrail, Spence was the last president to reside in

L&N Alco "Century" units waited to take over from C&EI GP35s arriving at Howell Yard, Evansville, with southbound all-piggyback train from Chicago in December 1968.

Louisville. He transferred in 1981 to Jacksonville to direct operations for the entire Family Lines system.

Passenger-wise, the 1970s marked the end of L&N's once extensive train services. On May 1, 1971, the road turned over its two remaining mainline trains to Amtrak (National Railroad Passenger Corporation), which on the same day took over most of the services of other U.S. railroads. A new Chicago-Florida train utilized L&N rails between Louisville-Montgomery for most of the decade, or until its discontinuance in October, 1979 (see Chapter 5, The Long Decline). From 1974 to 1978, a Midwest-Florida section of Auto-Train also used L&N between the same cities.

New Decade and New Corporation

The many changes of the 1970s, however, were but a prelude to the epochal changes that lay ahead for the L&N in the decade of the 1980s. First was creation of CSX Corporation, Inc., in November, 1980. The Richmond, Va.-based holding company brought together the parent companies of two "families" of railroads, the Chessie System (Baltimore & Ohio,

Chesapeake & Ohio, and Western Maryland) and Seaboard Coast Line Industries (SCL, L&N, Clinchfield, Georgia/West Point Route). A prospectus sent to stockholders of both parent companies declared:

"Merger of Chessie and Industries (SCL) will consolidate control of two complementary rail systems which geographically meet end to end. The combined companies will provide single rail-system service connecting the East and Midwest regions with the Southeast and create a unified rail network serving 22 states, the District of Columbia and Ontario, Canada. A major goal is to increase rail share of the transportation market through improved service and access to markets for shippers in the North and South. Managements(of Chessie and SCLI) believe that the merger will provide improved service to shippers, operating efficiencies and greater intermodal competition. …will permit more intensive utilization of equipment and facilities … and will mean improved profitability … and a stronger rail system in the East."

Richmond won out over Baltimore, Jacksonville, Lexington and Louisville as headquarters site for CSX. C&O and Seaboard had long maintained a major presence in the Virginia capital, and the two roads interchanged heavy traffic there as well as with the RF&P, which CSX was later to acquire. The close proximity of the nation's capital at Washington was also deemed important in the site selection.

Overall, Chessie stood to benefit from the merger by connecting its Northeastern service area with the faster growing Southeast, served by the Family Lines. SCLI/Family Lines, in turn, looked toward better access to the capital assets of Chessie to help it to continue expanding and modernizing. Both managements argued that the single-line service the two systems could henceforth provide would mitigate traditional problems of inter-road revenue allocations which often impeded solicitation and development of potential new traffic.

Architects forming CSX were Prime F. Osborn, SCLI's chairman, and Hays T. Watkins, president of the Chessie System. Messrs. Osborn and Watkins became chairman and president, respectively, of the new corporation, which laid claim to then owning the nation's largest rail system (upon Osborn's retirement in 1982, Watkins became Chairman and CEO). While the bulk of its revenues and assets were in railroading, CSX also owned interests in data processing, natural resources development, oil and gas, publishing, real estate and resort hotels, including the former C&O's famed Greenbrier, at White Sulphur Springs, W. Va.

At the outset, CSX business plans called for the two rail systems to operate separately but to coordinate operations as closely as possible. CSX's role was to provide the managing segment - or overall leadership - along with long range planning and policy creation for the two rail systems. Again, the ultimate goal was improvement of transportation services to all shippers. Some of the coordination improvements achieved by CSX during its formative years are cited in Chapter 7.

Seaboard System Railroad

An intermediate step in January, 1983, meanwhile, further solidified the Seaboard family side, as the five member roads—SCL, L&N, CRR, Georgia and West Point Route—officially merged on the first day of the new year to create Seaboard System Railroad. In addition to making the former SCLI rail holdings a legal entity with specific recognition in financial markets and the regulatory world, the action replaced the Family Lines nomenclature (itself never a corporate entity) with a single, strongly recognizable identity. Seaboard System's new president was Richard D. Sanborn, who had begun his rail career two decades before when he joined the law department of the former ACL.

In retrospect, Seaboard System's creation was inevitable, and the strategic coordination and consolidation projects that had been initiated in the 1970s under the Family Lines banner intensified after January 1, 1983, helping - as no doubt did the formation of CSX - to forge a stronger railroad more responsive to the demands of an increasingly competitive marketplace. For the five "family" member roads, however, it was the end, or finis, to their long years of development and struggle as individual railroad companies.

And, almost as swiftly as it came into being, Seaboard System Railroad itself lost identity. In late 1985, CSX announced major reorganization plans that completely reshaped and regrouped all of its holdings, including the two families of railroads. From those actions and other corporate changes which were to follow in the next several years was forged one large combined rail system, CSX Transportation. That rail mode was to be connected, corporately as well as operationally, with highway and waterway modes. As of this writing a decade later, CSX Transportation, the name given to the rail system, is the largest of CSX Corporation's properties and in 1995 ranked first nationally in operating revenues among other large rail systems.

Chessie and Seaboard System diesels,spotted together in 1983 at Queensgate Yard, Cincinnat, marked continuing coordination of operations, train services for larger CSX system.

One well might be saddened by the passing of long familiar corporate icons and nomenclature as they related to once favorite railroads, in this case, our old friend the L&N. ACL, SAL, Clinchfield, Georgia and West Point devotees likewise have sung and will continue singing their own particular laments. And yet, for the authors, there is reassurance in these realities, namely, that the territories carved out by L&N and the other "Family" roads were not abandoned or discarded but remain, being serviced most ably by the new successor, itself a viable rail property. Indeed, the very core railroad, be it L&N in ancestry or another, with its tracks, right-of-way, bridges, tunnels and more, continues to throb and pulse with train movements, just as intended. The legacy, in short, lives on.

Again, that's reassuring!

Tennessee Central

Oldest corporate component of the 257-mile long Tennessee Central was a company called the Nashville & Knoxville, which was organized by Alexander Crawford in the 1880s to tap the mineral wealth of the Cumberland Mountains east of Nashville. First trackage extended from Lebanon to Cookeville, then on to Monterey with a branch to Wilder in the 1890s. To gain access to Nashville, Crawford had hoped to connect at Lebanon with the 29-mile long Tennessee & Pacific, completed earlier (in 1871), but he was denied by the NC&StL, which had acquired the T&P soon after its completion.

In 1893, lawyer-turned-railroader Jere Baxter and his syndicate bought an interest in the Crawford properties, formed a new company, the Tennessee Central RR, to extend the line from Monterey on to Harriman and Knoxville as well as establish a west-end connection to Nashville and a terminus somewhere on the Tennessee River beyond. The Panic of 1893 and financial woes in its wake slowed Baxter, but after reorganization, Baxter and his TC finished the rugged mountainous segment from Monterey to Emory Gap in 1898, there connecting with the Southern's CNO&TP.

Rebuffed by the L&N/NC&StL monopoly in entering Nashville over the NC's Lebanon Branch, Baxter and his TC built their own line into the city in 1902, enabling TC and SR to inaugurate that May a through Nashville-Knoxville passenger service over the only direct route from middle Tennessee to Knoxville and the eastern counties. Also after 1900, an 83-mile extension was pushed west to Clarksville and Hopkinsville, Ky. But, again, the L&N-dominated animosity toward Baxter prevented a connection being built through Nashville, forcing TC to loop trackage around the south and west sides of the city!

On its Eastern Division (Nashville-Harriman), the TC encountered Cumberland Mountain topography even more rugged than that faced by the NC&StL between Nashville and Chattanooga. Heavy grades up to 3 percent, tortuous curves and several high trestles dominated much of the line's profile between Monterey, Crossville and Emory Gap. Coal, mined near Monterey and Wilder, was a leading TC commodity, although during World War II, much military traffic moved in and out of Fort Campbell, Ky., near Hopkinsville.

Because of the difficult profile and the sparsely populated counties it passed through, the TC was never very profitable, and as a result was reorganized several times. The road dieselized in 1952 and dropped passenger service in 1955, but even after those steps, it lost money most years.

John B. Allen/L&N Historical Society Collection

Tennessee Central 4-4-0 No. 3 was power for the first train to arrive at Rockwood, Tenn. on September 15, 1899.

In early 1968, TC management obtained permission to suspend service, and the road's last train ran on August 31. Four days later, the L&N took over the 135 mile Nashville-Crossville segment of TC's main line and began operating it under a temporary ICC permit. Then, in January 1969, the Commission authorized a three-way purchase of TC properties by the Illinois Central, Southern, and L&N which, as noted before, acquired the Nashville-Crossville portion. IC took over the Nashville-Hopkinsville line, while SR picked up Crossville-Harriman trackage. Some 40 former employees came to the L&N to continue running the line, and 20 locomotives and a number of cars were also purchased. During L&N's ownership, operations were conducted by a newly formed "Nashville & Eastern Branch," with additional help from L&N's own Nashville Division. L&N-successor Seaboard System later cut trackage back to Monterey, then sold the line in 1986 to a regional carrier which has since operated the road as the "Nashville & Eastern."

John B. Allen/L&N Historical Society Collection

Tennessee Central No. 553 was at Moneterey, Tennessee, on July 4, 1948.

Chicago and Eastern Illinois

For some years, the 950-mile long Chicago & Eastern Illinois advertised itself as the "Boulevard of Steel." Its main line, a major portion of which L&N acquired in 1969, ran straight as an arrow from the Chicago suburbs south to Danville, Ill., Terre Haute, Vincennes and Evansville, all in Indiana. In the wake of completion of L&N's bridge across the Ohio River at Henderson, Ky. in 1885, the two roads established a connection at Evansville (just across the river) and formed an important rail artery for passenger and freight traffic moving between the Midwest, Central South, Gulf Coast and Southeast.

Oldest antecedent of the C&EI was the Evansville & Illinois, which was chartered in 1849 to operate between Evansville and Vincennes, with train service beginning about 1853. Almost as old as the E&I was the Wabash R.R., organized in 1851 and opened in 1854 between Vincennes and Terre Haute or roughly parallel to the Wabash River (there was no relationship with the later Wabash Ry.)

Just after the end of the Civil War, a third C&EI predecessor, the Chicago, Danville & Vincennes gained a charter and built south from Dolton, Ill., to Danville, commencing operations in 1872.

The year before (1871), the Terre Haute-Danville segment was joined by steel rails by the recently formed (1869) Evansville, Terre Haute & Chicago. During the 1870s, that company, through several reorganizations and expansions, merged with the original Evansville and Wabash companies. In the meanwhile, the Chicago, Danville & Vincennes itself reorganized, adopting the now familiar C&EI name and, in 1880, leasing Danville-Terre Haute-Evansville trackage from the former ETH&C. Thus was created C&EI's so-called "Eastern Line." The new company went on to later build a line south from Danville through Mt. Vernon, Ill., to Thebes and Joppa. Trackage and connections into the St. Louis gateway were consummated in the early 1900s.

The C&EI was variously controlled by the Frisco and the rail empire of the Van Sweringen Brothers (C&O, Missouri Pacific, Nickel Plate, Pere Marquette, etc.), between 1902-1940. Meanwhile, C&EI, especially from the 1920s on, participated with L&N, NC&StL and other southeastern roads in operating an extensive through passenger service from Chicago to Atlanta and Florida, as will be more fully described in later chapters. That cooperation led to streamlining several trains, beginning in 1940, and offering even faster service. Then, in the early 1960s, as piggyback began to lure truck trailers back to rails, C&EI and L&N launched an expedited trailer-train service between Chicago, Nashville and Atlanta, a service that has been extended to Florida and has since produced great increases in intermodal traffic.

In 1961, L&N expressed interest in the C&EI by purchasing a minority stock interest, Mopac previously having commenced merger talks with the line. In 1965, the ICC approved Mopac's application to take over the C&EI but with the proviso that negotiations with L&N also be undertaken for sale of the Evansville line. Agreement between the two lines was reached in 1969, enabling L&N to purchase 287 miles of C&EI (Woodland Junction-Evansville, also the Mt. Vernon, Ind., branch) for about $40 million. Ownership of the double-track from Villa Grove north to Dolton came to be shared with Mopac, with L&N obtaining operating rights into Greater Chicago over the Belt Railway of Chicago and the Chicago & Western Indiana. Also included in the sale were 48 locomotives and nearly 1,500 freight cars and cabooses.

"Acquisition of the C&EI," declared L&N President Kendall, "permits us to offer and provide improved single-line service from the Great Lakes to the Gulf and Southeast...as well as to those cities between Chicago and Evansville formerly served by the C&EI. ...This new section of our main line can be expected to become one of the most important parts of the L&N system."

With heavy Pacific No. 1020 at the helm, C&EI'S northbound *Dixie Limited* rolled through 79th Street on Chicago's south side in June 1940. During the previous night L&N, NC&StL forwarded the train from Atlanta to Evansville.

Mr. Kendall was right on target with his prophecy, as the passage of time has proven!

Monon Railroad

For more than 120 years, the Monon and its predecessors served Indiana, or from the late 1840s to 1971 and merger into the larger L&N system. While not the Hoosier State's earliest rail line, the Monon (or more correctly, its antecedent New Albany & Salem) nevertheless was the first to build the entire length of the state, from Southern Indiana to Lake Michigan. Wrote one historian, the road was "the first faltering finger of transport which crept out of the Ohio Valley to carry settlers into the more fertile counties of the north. ..."

The Monon story began in the 1840s with James Brooks, a New Albany banker, who with other Southern Indiana business leaders saw the limitations of the Ohio River at their doorstep and that of regional wagon roads; instead, they envisioned opportunities to the north in the agricultural and mineral potential of Central Indiana and the Great Lakes. In 1847, the men acquired the abandoned right-of-way of an old macadam road being projected upstate to Salem and Crawfordsville and obtained a charter for the New Albany & Salem Railroad. Construction began in 1848; by 1851, the NA&S had reached Salem, then Bedford and Bloomington in 1853.

While Indianapolis initially was in NA&S sights, a more ambitious plan looked beyond, to Lake Michigan. That plan was encouraged by, one, completion of a railroad between Crawfordsville and Lafayette, and two, the ambitions of the Michigan Central to reach Chicago. During 1852-3, and using its own charter rights, the NA&S helped the Michigan road build across Northern Indiana and on to the Windy City. In return, NA&S got capital enough to acquire outright the Crawfordsville-Lafayette line, build a connection from it south to Bloomington to tie in with its own trackage from New Albany, and finally, push rails north from Lafayette to Michigan City. The last-named construction included a 65-mile long tangent, between Monon and Michigan City.

On June 24, 1854, track forces drove the final spike at Putnamville, near Greencastle to complete the last stretch of unfinished rail. On July 3, the first through train traveled south over the completed route all the way from Lake Michigan to the Ohio River, and a big celebration the next day at New Albany marked formal opening of the line. Total cost to build and equip the NA&S - $6 million.

Traffic, slow to build up during the 1850s, improved late in the decade with opening of a Cincinnati-Chicago route that utilized NA&S tracks north of Lafayette and with completion (in October 1859) of the L&N main line from Louisville south to Nashville. Recognizing the growing importance of New Albany's larger neighbor just across river, management, also in 1859, renamed its road the Louisville, New Albany & Chicago. Indeed, the Louisville tie-in would prove to be beneficial, traffic-wise, with L&N's later expansion into the Central South and Gulf Coast.

Business-wise, a dismal 15 years that followed the Civil War gave way to brighter times in the 1880s, as the LNA&C gained its own access to the Windy City in 1884. It did so, by purchasing the incompleted Chicago & Indianapolis Air Line Railway and extending trackage from Dyer to Hammond. Trackage rights, also secured in 1884, took LNA&C through trains from Hammond into downtown Chicago. And, some 80 miles of the former C&IAL from Delphi to Indianapolis were finished, to put the LNA&C into the developing Chicago-Indy corridor. The road's route map hereafter took on an "X" configuration, with the two main lines crossing at the small community of Monon (much later to give its name to the line).

Additional growth in the late 1880s to the early 1900s brought into LNA&C ownership the 18-mile branch from Orleans to the famed resorts at French Lick and West Baden Springs, in Southern Indiana, as well as the coal-producing Midland branch, running from Wallace Junction to Victoria and several spurs to serve the limestone industry around Bedford. Meanwhile, between 1889-90, the LNA&C made a brief foray into Kentucky after establishing connections with the Louisville Southern (which it helped extend to Lexington). The Eastern Kentucky coal fields were sought, which LNA&C hoped to reach,

L&N Collection, University Of Louisville Archives

Assembled in New Albany, Indiana, high wheeled *Admiral* pulled Monon predecessor Louisville, New Albany & Chicago's passenger trains back in the 1860s and '70s.

J. F. Bennett/L&N Collection, University Of Louisville Archives

Monon heavy Mikado No. 551 symbolically gave way to an oncoming Monon fast freight behind new F3 dieselsat Gosport, In. In late 1940s, Monon became first major U.S. railroad to dieselize train operations.

over LS rails and those of the just finished Richmond, Nicholasville, Irvine & Beattyville ("Riney-B", to come into L&N's ownership after 1900). A change in management dumped the project, and after reorganization later in the 1890s, the LNA&C became the Chicago, Indianapolis & Louisville (or CI&L). After 1900, the L&N and Southern each acquired a minority interest in the line's stock.

Notwithstanding its financial "ups and downs" during the 'teens, '20s and '30s, the Monon continued to invest heavily in equipment and fixed-property improvements to maintain a reputation for quality service. Especially noteworthy was its vigorous modernization after World War II under the leadership of its president, John W. Barriger III. A major facet of the renovation had Monon almost overnight replacing steam power with diesels, becoming in the late '40s the first U.S. line to fully dieselize.

Barriger also spruced up Monon's passenger trains by rebuilding a fleet of war-surplus hospital cars into streamlined equipment to replace aging equipment; hundreds of new freight cars also went into service throughout the 1950s and 60s, and significant roadway improvements—new bridges, rail replacement, and curve and grade reductions—were undertaken to upgrade Monon physical properties and improve service.

As the rail merger movement nationally gathered momentum in the 1960s, it was inevitable that the Monon, with its strategic location across Indiana, would become a factor in the movement. By the late 1960s, with L&N aligned to receive C&EI's Evansville Line, it was expected that the Monon would join forces with other railroads, notably Southern. But, in 1968, the L&N and Monon agreed on a merger proposal which the ICC found to be in the public interest. Ultimately, the proposal led to formal merger on August 1, 1971.

From L&N's perspective, acquisition of the Monon gave it a second entrance to Chicago as well as an alternate north-south route from the Ohio Valley to Lake Michigan. L&N also gained access to Indianapolis, Indiana's largest city and capital. Grains, produced in central and northern Indiana, were high on Monon's freight commodity mix, and prospects of gaining longer hauls into the South for that traffic further enhanced merger prospects. The Monon's position was well expressed by its then-President, Samuel T. Brown, who just prior to the merger told stockholders "we feel that the pride and spirit of our railroad will follow merger into the L&N and greatly contribute to realizing the potential of the combined systems."

J. Parker Lamb

From Indiana corn fields and Tennessee hill country to Alabama pinelands and Gulf Coast waters, L&N Land "geography" was striking in its diversity. Southbound freight traversed deep cut on main line near Brentwood, Tenn., just south of Nashville in August 1964.

Some Corporate and Geographic Considerations

The L&N in its full geographic maturity (1971) consisted of 6,574 route miles of road serving 13 midwestern and southeastern states: Alabama, Florida, Georgia, Illinois, Indiana, Kentucky, Louisiana, Mississippi, Missouri, North Carolina, Ohio, Tennessee, and Virginia. Grand total of all tracks, including second mains, passing and yard tracks came to over 8,000 miles. In route mileages, Kentucky led the states, with 1,800 miles of L&N trackage, followed by Alabama, with some 1,100 miles, and Tennessee, with about 900 miles.

General Offices in Louisville

For most of its 132 years as a railroad company, the L&N was headquartered in Louisville, Ky. From the mid-1850s on, company officers and their staffs were housed in several different buildings downtown, beginning with the combination freight and passenger depot at 9th and Broadway, designed and completed in 1857 by L&N's then chief engineer, Albert Fink. Soon after, however, some offices were moved to a building at Main and Bullitt Streets, then (in 1877) to a larger building several blocks away, at the corner of Second and Main.

But, by the beginning of a new century, yet more administrative space was needed for the headquarters staff of an L&N which, by then, ran from the Ohio and Mississippi Valleys to the Gulf Coast. In 1902, in the very same block on which was erected the company's first station in the 1850s, excavation began for a new 11-story brick office building. Five years later, in January 1907, officers and employees transferred from 2nd and Main to 9th and Broadway and into spacious new quarters at 9th and Broadway. An annex that exactly matched the architecture of the original 1907 wing was completed in 1930. The handsome Louisville building, one of the largest in the nation in use by a single railroad, came to serve L&N and its successors for the next half-century.

With consolidation of many L&N and SCL departments in Jacksonville after 1980, L&N began to lease some floors to the Commonwealth of Kentucky's Department of Human Resources, and in 1984, the state purchased the building but allowed the railroad to

L&N Historical Society Collection

L&N's General Office Building at 908 West Broadway in Louisville was thought to have been one of the largest building in the nation occupied by a single railroad for its headquarters. The distinctive neon "L&N" sign was added in the mid-1950s and still brightens the Louisville skyline at night, even though the road ceased to exist after 1983. Now owned by the Commonwealth of Kentucky, the building houses state offices.

lease space on some floors. Last remaining CSX-T departments moved away in 1988 to locations elsewhere in the city. Happily, the large illuminated "L&N" sign on the east end of the building, installed in 1959, remains to this day, and because the Louisville GOB had became such a local landmark, the state and its departments continue to refer to the structure as the "L&N Building."

Major departments housed in the Louisville GOB were: Accounting & Taxation, Executive, Finance, Law, Operating and Traffic. Accounting also included Comptroller, Internal Auditing/Accounting Procedures and Tax. Within Law were the Claims, Commerce and General Divisions. Operating, in turn, divided into Engineering, Mechanical, Transportation and Personnel, while traffic took in freight and Passenger Sales as well as Coal, Intermodal, Industrial Development, Marketing Research and Pricing. From the mid-1960s on, an operations center was also based at the Louisville GOB to monitor system operations and deploy motive power where needed. As of 1971, Louisville GOB employment stood at some 1,500 men and women.

L&N Served The South- and Nation

Sizeable staffs served the railroad at its diverse division headquarters as well, in Atlanta, Birmingham, Cincinnati, Corbin, Evansville, Knoxville, Mobile and Nashville (The Louisville Division superintendent and staff were based at Union Station at 10th & Broadway until moving into the GOB in 1978). Staff also operated major yards in the above cities (Atlanta, Cincinnati, Louisville and Nashville had separate "Terminal" jurisdictions, each with a superintendent) as well as smaller yards and terminals elsewhere on the system.

For many decades, freight and passenger sales offices were maintained in many large on-line and off-line cities, including San Francisco and Seattle. Also, L&N's long-time Vice President-Finance W. J. McDonald and staff kept an office on Wall Street in New York where, traditionally, the chairman of the board (ACL's and L&N's) resided. At full maturity, system trackage connected regions of the industrial Midwest, North and Central South with the important Gulf Coast ports of Mobile, New Orleans, Pascagoula and Pensacola. Especially

David Oroszi

L&N's Atlanta Division was steeped in Civil War history; southbound freight passed marker for grave of unknown Confederate soldier near Allatoona, Ga., in 1981

significant to L&N was the fact that the Central South, Southeast and Gulf Coast experienced great growth during the three decades following World War II. Commodities and products originating from these regions included automotive products, coal, paper and pulpwood, chemicals, household, steel and steel products, lumber, and a wide assortment of grains, farm and food products.

In terms of operations, the L&N System was divided into geographic divisions, each covering specific regions and each headed by a superintendent (later renamed division manager) and staff. A trend throughout L&N's more recent history tended to consolidate smaller divisions into fewer, larger units, and by the 1970s, each division acquired the name of its headquarters city. Also over the decades, some routes were swapped back and forth between divisions to equalize mileages and territories. As of 1976, there were seven operating divisions, and their routes, territories and geography are briefly described below.

1. *Atlanta Division:*

The Atlanta Division formed an important coal and intermodal route, with a main line extending from Nashville to Atlanta via Chattanooga. Branches served Sparta, Shelbyville, Tracy City, Pikeville, and Fayetteville, all in Tennessee, and Huntsville, Alabama (Most were abandoned or sold to shortline operators, beginning in 1970s). L&N's original Knoxville route (old Atlanta, Knoxville & Northern or Etowah-Blue Ridge-Marietta line) fed into the divisional domain at Marietta, Ga., and just to the north, at

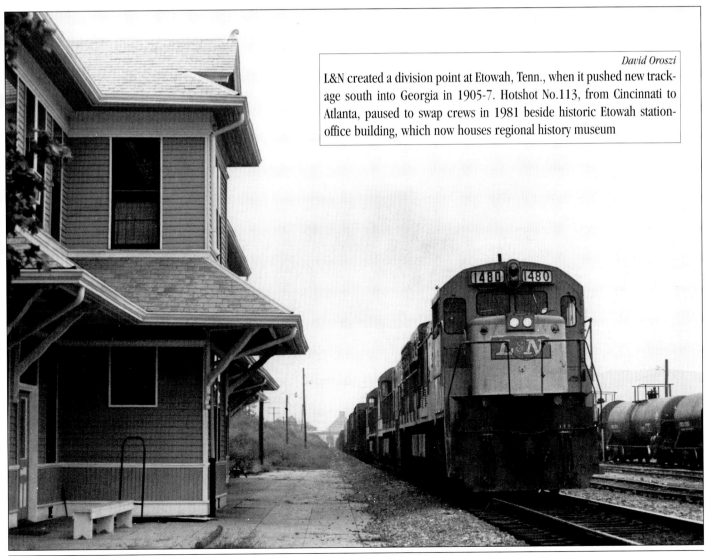

David Oroszi

L&N created a division point at Etowah, Tenn., when it pushed new trackage south into Georgia in 1905-7. Hotshot No.113, from Cincinnati to Atlanta, paused to swap crews in 1981 beside historic Etowah station-office building, which now houses regional history museum

43

L&N Collection, University of Louisville Archives

L&N cut through several North Alabama hills to create new Boyles Yard in 1957-9. Big hump yard lay just north of Birmingham, cost $12-million to build, the original yard was to the south.

Cartersville, the more direct and newer line, also from Etowah, joined the main line from Chattanooga. Trackage rights brought L&N trains to and from metro Atlanta.

Prior to the 1957 L&N-NC&StL merger, the Nashville-Chattanooga segment comprised NC's old Chattanooga Division, with the Atlanta Division governing the Georgia state-owned Western & Atlantic (Chattanooga-Atlanta). During the 1960s, the entire division was known as the "Western & Atlantic."

CTC machines formerly in Cowan, Tn., and Dalton, Ga., were consolidated in Atlanta by 1975.

The former W&A main stem (Atlanta-Chattanooga) progressed in a northwesterly direction from Atlanta and the North Georgia Piedmont Plateau to intersect Appalachian and Blue Ridge Mountain ranges. Beyond Chattanooga, the division's main line likewise intersected several Appalachian ranges, most specifically the Cumberlands, through which the pioneering Nashville & Chattanooga successfully tunneled in 1852. The division and several of its branches also utilized the broad valleys which lay between the mountain ranges as well as part of the valley cut by the Tennessee River. Between Etowah and Copperhill, the K&A "Old Line" (original Knoxville-Atlanta route) negotiated Bald Mountain by means of the 8,000 foot Hiwassee Loop, third longest rail loop. The loop and a sharp curve near Tate, Ga., gave the line its "Hook and Eye" moniker.

Major Terminals:

Atlanta- Tilford Yard (hump), opened 1957, incorporating much of former NC&StL Hills Park Yard; expanded 1964; Union Station, opened 1930, demolished 1974. Chattanooga-Wauhatchie Yard, opened 1961, replacing former NC&StL Cravens Yard; Union Station, built 1880s, demolished 1974.

2. Birmingham Division:

L&N's so-called "back bone" comprised much of this large division, embracing as it did the main line running south from Nashville via Lewisburg and Birmingham to Montgomery. Between Brentwood, Tn., and North Athens, Ala., the Nashville & Decatur Subdivision with the NF&S branch from Columbia to Florence, Ala., paralleled the main stem to the west. Other branches radiated from Birmingham to tap the coal and iron ore-producing areas of North Alabama. These included the Alabama Mineral "circle" route, via Gadsden, Anniston and Calera and the Birmingham Mineral, running southwest to Tuscaloosa. Division headquarters and CTC machine were at 4100 Vanderbilt Road in Birmingham.

Birmingham Division geography varied considerably, from more level terrain of Alabama's Gulf Coastal Plain around and just north of Montgomery to the hillier extensions of the Appalachians, which the main line bisected between Birmingham and Hartselle, Ala. Southbound trains faced the division's ruling grade up Sand Mountain, between

J. Parker Lamb

The Birmingham Division main trunk bisected the hilly extension of the Appalachians which lay in North Alabama. A U25B/F7 lashup worked a northbound fast freight through a deep cut near Cullman, Ala., in August, 1965.

Long a separate operating entity, Cincinnati Terminals fed, received traffic from the Corbin and Louisville Division main stems, also interchanged with connecting railroads. With Cincinnati's skyline as a backdrop, two U25Bs brought piggybacks across Chessie's Ohio river bridge and into Covington, Ky.

Hartselle and Cullman. A less difficult profile existed northward from Decatur, on the Tennessee River, and in the Appalachian plateau, on to Tennessee's Highland Rim and into the Nashville Basin. L&N extensively upgraded the old South & North Alabama main stem of the division between 1911-14, reducing grades and curves and installing double track from North Athens south to Calera. The Lewisburg Subdivision (Brentwood-Athens), which avoided the curves of the older N&D, was also built at that time.

Major Terminals:

Birmingham-Boyles Yard (hump), expanded and modernized, 1959; Union Station, opened 1960, now used by Amtrak (replaced older station built in 1887).

Montgomery-S&N Yard; Union Station, built 1896, closed 1979 after discontinuance of *Floridian*. Smaller flat yards at Columbia and Mt. Pleasant Tn., and Decatur, Al., site of former Albany Shop complex.

3. *Corbin Division:*

The Corbin Division was a mid-1970s creation, consolidating all coal-hauling operations on the east side of the system. New headquarters (with computer-assisted CTC) were built at Corbin, bringing together supervision and staff from the former Cincinnati, Cumberland Valley, Eastern Kentucky and Knoxville Divisions. The new division embraced the Cincinnati-Knoxville-Etowah main line (former "KY" and K&A Division ter-

Rugged Appalachian terrain enhanced portrait of L&N, SCL diesels at Cumberland Mountain Tunnel near Cowan, Tenn., as C. Norman Beasley, L&N's chief photographer, restaged 1940s NC&StL familiar promo stunt 30 years later. SCL GP-40 occupied Nashville-Chattanooga main line; L&N GP38-2, above tunnel mouth, was on Tracy City Branch.

L&N's largest freight classification yard, DeCoursey, lay along the Licking River just south of Covington, KY. Expanded and upgraded in 1962-4, yard boasted twin humps for north- and southbound traffic.

ritories), together with old "EK" trackage from the Hazard-area coal fields west through Lexington to near Louisville, also from Corbin through the Southeastern Kentucky coal fields to Harlan, Lynch, Middlesboro and Norton (old "CV" routes).

Much of the new division (and its predecessor divisions) lay in the foothills of the Appalachians, and the many curves and heavy grades, especially east from Corbin and south to Knoxville, made operations far more difficult than did more moderate profiles elsewhere on the system. Nonetheless, L&N civil engineers took advantage of the several major

waterways (and their valleys) which flowed out of the region. The North Fork of the Kentucky River offered a mostly downgrade path for the former EK, as did the Cumberland River, to the south, for trains of the former CV Division. And, from Paris north to the Ohio Valley at Covington, a gentle downhill profile was provided by the Licking River for coal tonnages rolling off both the CV and EK and destined for the Cincinnati gateway.

Major Terminals:

Corbin-East, West Yards (upgraded 1986-7, with addition of new diesel shop replacing steam era shop); Cincinnati/Coving-ton-

L&N's former Eastern Kentucky Division (later Corbin) followed Kentucky River and tributaries for almost 200 miles, nature provided the railroad a mostly downhill profile to favor northbound loaded coal trains, represented by steam-era run near Beattyville, KY., in the 1940s.

Terminal district part of Corbin Division and included DeCoursey Yard. Its first hump opened 1940; yard greatly expanded with second hump, modernized, 1964; closed 1984 and all operations moved to Chessie's Queensgate Yard (hump), Cincinnati. Cincinnati Union Terminal (L&N was one of CUT owner railroads), opened 1933, closed 1971, with part of concourse demolished; Rotunda saved, and building again used by Amtrak. Knoxville Union Station, opened 1904, closed 1968, later became upscale restaurant for city's Worlds Fair. Smaller flat yards were located at Etowah, Hazard, Loyall (Harlan), West Knoxville, West Lexington and Ravenna.

Just four days before Christmas 1964, former Cumberland Valley Division time freight No. 66 on Norton, Va.- Corbin, Ky., run headed out of Appalachia, Va., having just passed through Bee Rock Tunnel, division's shortest bore.

4. Evansville Division:

This division formed a rough "X", its major lines extending from the Chicago and St. Louis gateways through the headquarters city to Louisville and Nashville. Another secondary route ran south from Owensboro to Russellville, being intersected midway in its length by an east-west branch tapping the Western Kentucky coal fields. Other branches served Mt. Vernon and Shawneetown, in Southern Indiana and Illinois, respectively. The division also possesses the L&N's longest bridge, the three-and-one-half-mile Ohio River bridge and its approaches, between Evansville and Henderson, and the second longest tunnel, a 4,621-footer, at Ridgecrest, Tn., just north of Nashville.

The Henderson Subdivision (Evansville-Nashville) carried the heaviest traffic load of the four principal subdivisions, trains and ton-nages flowing to and from the Chicago (former C&EI trackage) and St. Louis "subs," much of that traffic being Midwest-Southeast grains and intermodal as well as Western Kentucky coal moving north. The Evansville-Louisville line was formerly the Louisville, Henderson & St. Louis Ry., acquired by the L&N in 1929. As previously noted, the Owensboro & Nashville (O&N) sub ran south through Western Kentucky, intersecting the coal-hauling Madisonville, Hartford & Eastern sub (MH&E). For years based in Union Station downtown, division dispatchers, staff and supervisors in the mid 1970s moved out to a new building at Howell Yard (at the same time former C&EI dispatchers were brought down from Danville, Ill.).

Generally flat fertile farmlands characterized much of the Midwestern expanse encountered by Evansville Division trackage in Illinois, Indiana and Western Kentucky, also

L&N Collection, University of Louisville Archives
The Evansville Division claimed L&N's longest bridge, the three-and-a-half mile Henderson Bridge across the Ohio River. A Chicago-Atlanta all-trailer train ascended the north approach to the Bridge in the mid-1960s.

Biggest yard on division was at Howell, on Evansville's southwest side. Yard handled trains to and from four subdivisions - Chicago (ex-C&EI), St.Louis, Henderson and LH&StL. In 1967 aerial, train yard stretched from upper left to lower right; roundhouse, car shop were to right.

R. D. Acton Sr.

On former C&EI trackage, an Evansville-bound fast freight clumped across Conrail's Indianapolis-St. Louis mainline at Terre Haute, In. Haley Tower's operator eye-balled the power and rack cars of the L&N hotshot.

accounting for the vast grain tonnages originating on the division. Midwest plains, of course, gave way to foothills and lowlands in southern sections of Illinois and Indiana, calling for moderate grades and curves, which also were found in Western Kentucky's Pennyroyal Plateau (through which the HD and O&N subs passed). By contrast, surveyors of the LH&StL predecessor took advantage of the Ohio River Valley and its flood plain to locate their trackage between Henderson, Owensboro and Louisville.

Major Terminals:

Danville, Ill. - Brewer Yard, former C&EI flat yard, upgraded by L&N in 1976; Oaklawn

Shops, former C&EI heavy repair facility, closed and sold to private industry; East St. Louis, Ill., yard, closed early 1980s, when operations moved to adjacent B&O Cone Yard. Evansville-Howell Yard, expanded in early 1980s after former C&EI Wansford Yard closed. Union Station, opened 1904, closed 1971 and building later torn down.

Madisonville, Ky.- Atkinson Yard, expanded 1963 to serve western Kentucky coal fields, unit train operations. Smaller flat yards were at Owensboro (Doyle) and Hawesville (Skillman), both on LH&StL Subdivision in Kentucky.

L&N General Office Building, Union Station, freight house and supporting yards were located on West Broadway between 9th and 11th Streets, in downtown Louisville.

5. Louisville Division:

The "Genesis" Division was closely tied to the 19th century history and development of the L&N. In terms of origins the division embraced the original Louisville-Nashville main line, along with the Bardstown, Glasgow, Greensburg, Lebanon and Scottsville Branches (most of their mileage also being in Kentucky). Once also part of the division, the so-called "Memphis Line" (Bowling Green-Clarksville-Memphis) was given to the Nashville Division after the NC&StL merger, in 1957. However, that loss was offset by the addition, in 1971, of the Monon and its Louisville-Chicago main stem, together with its Indianapolis, Michigan City and other shorter branches in Indiana.

Even more recently and as a result of the Corbin Division formation in the mid 1970s, Louisville picked up the important "Short Line" Subdivision (Louisville-Covington). Based for years at Union Station, division staff also in the 1970s transferred to new quarters (and a new computer-assisted CTC machine) on the first floor, west wing, of the Louisville GOB.

Excepting the ruling Muldraugh Hill and Tennessee Ridge grades, the Louisville Division main stem took advantage of the mostly level uplands of Kentucky's Pennyroyal Plateau. More broken terrain, of course, was encountered by the line in Middle Tennessee as it dropped through the Highland Rim to

C. Norman Beasley/L&N Collection, University of Louisville Archives

During the 1960s and 70s, L&N accomplished many freight car upgrading programs in one-mile long "Shops 3 and 4" at South Louisville. In November 1963, opentop hoppers advanced through 29 work stations of rebuild program, right, while miscellaneous fabrication work on frames progressed, at left.

Wm. C. Tayse/L&N Collection, University of Louisville Archives

&N's system car and locomotive shops were based at Louisville, operating from 1905 until their closure in 1987. Locomotive repairs were concentrated in horizontal building, above left, freight cars in long vertical structure, to right.

Wm. C. Tayse/L&N Collection,
University of Louisville Archives

Although encountering hilly terrain in southern Kentucky and Middle Tennessee, Louisville Division also possessed long stretches of tangent track across upland plateaus of South Central Kentucky. On double track near Lebanon Junction, Signal Maintainer Ollie Larkin posted conditional stop sign (part of radio flagging procedures) to protect track crew working nearby

Nashville. The Lebanon Branch also ran into hillier going as it pushed southeastward toward the Appalachian Plateau and foothills. One might have assumed that builders of the Short Line (Louisville-Cincy) would have utilized the Ohio River valley basin much of the way, but instead they located the SL route well south of the flood plain to intersect sharp ridges and steep valleys cut by streams: hence the SL's profile matched a roller coaster much of the way!

Major Terminals:

Louisville- Osborn Yard (hump), opened 1977, incorporating part of old Strawberry Yard; South Louisville Shops, opened 1905, replacing older pre-Civil War era shops downtown; closed 1987 and buildings demolished 1994. Union Station, opened 1891, closed 1976 and sold to city's transit authority.

Smaller flat yards at Bowling Green, Ky., and Bloomington, West Lafayette and South Hammond, all in Indiana and former Monon facilities (Lafayette was also site of Monon's principal shops)

Charles B. Castner/L&N Collection, University of Louisville Archives
Picturesque Bardstown Branch ran through Kentucky "knob" country to reach several distilleries; its trains brought in barrels and grains, hauled out bottled spirits. No. 35 spotted a car of malt at Limestone Springs in 1963. Part of line now is owned and operated by R. C. Corman Railroad.

Wm. C. Tayse/L&N Collection, University of Louisville Archives

L&N's only seaport division tapped five Gulf Coast cities and their port facilities: New Orleans, Gulfport, Pascagoula, Mobile and Pensacola. Cargoes were transferred from boxcars to waiting ocean ship at Mobile's Alabama State Docks.

Montgomery-to-Mobile tonnage got fast ride southward from the Alabama capital city behind white-flagged F7 duo in June 1954. Level to rolling terrain characterized much of 180-mile "M&M Sub," its antecedents dating back to just before and after Civil War.

6. Mobile Division:

L&N's southernmost division included the main line from Montgomery via Mobile to New Orleans, as well as important secondary routes, which extended southward from Selma, Ala., to Pensacola and eastward to Chattahoochee, also in Florida. Branches also served Foley and Myrtlewood, in Alabama, and Florala and Graceville, in Florida. Until recently, the division was known as the MNO&P (Mobile, New Orleans & Pensacola) and for many years was headquartered in Mobile (on the second floor of the newer passenger station since the 1950s).

As with other divisions, Mobile Division "subs" derived their titles from the several predecessors, including the former Montgomery & Mobile (M&M), New Orleans, Mobile & Texas, Pensacola R.R. (Flomaton-Pensacola) and Pensacola & Atlantic (P&A), which built east across the Florida Panhandle in 1881-3. The generally flat terrain of the East Gulf Coastal Plain allowed for a mostly level profile, with gentle curves and grades for most subdivisions. Heavily forested, the region has also contributed much paper, pulpwood and wood products traffic.

Trackage between Mobile and New Orleans lay at sea level on fills and pilings and at water's edge much of that distance and intersected numerous bayous and inland waterways. Such conditions presented special operating challenges, particularly to L&N's engineering staff. Well over 20 miles of the division were also on bridges and trestles, many of the latter timber, requiring special treatment to protect against Teredo and sea rot. Over the decades, the L&N extensively upgraded major bridge structures at Bay St. Louis, Biloxi, Mobile, Pascagoula, Pearl River, Chef Menteur and Rigolets as well as improved smaller trestles and culverts. Similar betterments also took place on the P&A sub across West Florida.

Major Terminals:

Mobile-Sibert Yard, opened 1929, upgraded 1966; passenger station, built 1955, closed 1979 but later periodically used by Amtrak.

Montgomery-S&N Yard; Union Station, opened 1896, also used by ACL, West Point Route and, after 1971, by Amtrak; New

Orleans-Gentilly Yard, built 1908, expanded 1960s with intermodal facilities; Union Station (NOUPT), opened 1954, with L&N as one of owning railroads; now used by Amtrak. L&N's older Canal Street Station (built 1901) closed 1954, demolished 1956.

Pensacola-Goulding Yard, opened 1930s replacing smaller yard at Wright St. downtown; Muscogee Wharf, other port facilities, sold to Port Authority; L&N Marine Terminal preserved by city. Union Station, opened 1913, closed 1971, now part of luxury hotel complex. Smaller flat yards at Flomaton, Al., Pascagoula, Miss.

7. Nashville Division:

The Nashville Division linked its namesake city with west Tennessee and the Memphis gateway. Branch lines ran to Centerville and Union City, both in Tennessee, also to Paducah, Ky. Heart of the division was the 90-mile Nashville-Bruceton trunk, which was part of the former NC&StL's mainline to Memphis (which continued to the southwest, via Lexington, Jackson and Somerville).

After the 1957 merger, L&N added its own Memphis Line (Bowling Green-Clarksville-

J. Parker Lamb

Vast Nashville Terminal track changes from just after turn of century also provided by-pass route to the east of downtown Nashville for L&N freight trains. Years later (in 1965), a northbound freight on the bypass crossed Shelby Park and the Cumberland River.

The many bridge structures of the Mobile Division (and predecessor MNO&P Division) required continual maintenance, and for some years L&N maintained a creosoting plant at Gautier, Miss., just west of Pascagoula to protect crossties and bridge timbers against *Teredo Navalis*, a sea worm which feasted on wood structures.

McKenzie-Memphis) to the division and began routing through Nashville-Memphis freights via McKenzie and its own more populous route south of that point to the Memphis gateway. Trackage between Clarksville and Paris was later abandoned when the Tennessee River bridge at Danville was closed (the drawspan and several other spans went to Bridgeport, Ala.). Portions of the former NC&StL main between Bruceton-Memphis were later abandoned, although Jackson continued to be served, accessed over the IC (later NS) from Milan. Although the superintendent and his staff maintained offices in Nashville, NC&StL (and later L&N) dispatchers were long based in the key junction point of Bruceton. L&N's pre-merger "Memphis Line" dispatchers resided in Paris, Tn.

West Tennessee also lay in the Gulf Coastal and Mississippi Alluvial Plains, allowing for much tangent trackage and generally level profiles on the Nashville Division's main routes. East of Bruceton, however, the line crossed the Tennessee River at New Johnsonville, then traversed the elevated Highland Rim, to drop into the Nashville Basin. Because of its "hill and dale" character, that segment of the division was nicknamed "The Windy."

Major Terminals: Bruceton yard, at junction of former NC&StL's Nashville-Union City, Paducah-Memphis routes.

Memphis-Leewood Yard, on northeast side of city, replaced older freight terminal near N. Main St. and 1880s passenger station there; NC&StL trains made up in smaller yard next to Union Station downtown, filled out at Aulon, but after L&N merger moved into Leewood; Union Station, opened 1913 and used by both L&N, NC&StL passenger trains; closed and demolished, late 1960s.

Nashville-Kayne Avenue Yard, in downtown "railroad gulch," site of former NC&StL train yard, in use today; Radnor Yard, opened by L&N in 1918, expanded and modernized to become first hump yard in 1954 (by then also handling all NC&StL trains); Union Station, opened 1900, closed 1979; building now upscale hotel; former NC&StL West Nashville Shops, opened 1890, closed 1959 after L&N merger; buildings demolished.

David & Jill Oroszi

By the 1970s, L&N's Nashville-Memphis main line had become busy run-through corridor with the former Missouri Pacific. Run-through Freight #588, with Mopac power, sped through cut near New Johnsonville, Tenn., on its way west to Memphis Gateway in June 1980.

Steve Patterson

Near Union Station in downtown Memphis, two EMD switchers deliver a transfer cut from L&N's Leewood Yard on the north side of the city to a connecting railroad in June 1963. Advent of run-through freights later in decade reduced frequency and need for such runs.

Everett N. Young

Three Alco C420s rumbled out of Chenowee Tunnel near Yeadon, Ky., on the EK Sub with empties for Southeast Coal Co. tipples; April 1978.

A System Appreciation

Joseph G. Kerr was the Assistant to L&N's Vice President—Traffic in the 1920s. Little known or remembered today, Mr. Kerr nonetheless performed a valued service during that decade, representing as he did the carrier before the Interstate Commerce Commission in Washington, D.C.

Through his presentations of history, operations and traffic, he argued for proper valuation and worth of the railroad and its properties. Happily, some of Mr. Kerr's ICC testimony survives, as does a detailed chronology of the railroad's development, which he also prepared in 1926. Although written in a past age, Mr. Kerr's remarks are still appropriate to this review of L&N progress and achievement.

In describing how the L&N evolved into a unified system, Mr. Kerr wrote, "...the great majority of the independent lines acquired by the L&N before or after 1890 through purchase or lease had not been successfully and profitably operated as independent railroads, and in my judgement but few of them could today (1926) be profitably so operated except possibly on basis of a materially higher level of

freight and passenger rates...and sacrificing the development of the country. All of these independent railroads, when rehabilitated, properly extended...and developed, and receiving the benefits of a coordinated and efficient single operating system, were and are of much greater value than they were when operated separately......As parts of such a system, they are of much value."

Mr. Kerr continued: "From the building of the original line (between Louisville and Nashville in the 1850s), there followed a gradual extension by wise construction of new lines or prudent acquirement of old lines, a consistent development of the local resources of the territories served ... and development of local and through traffic for all parts of the system....Welded together, the various lines became of inestimable value to each other. Fully coordinated, the whole system of lines handled a much larger freight and passenger traffic and with greater efficiency than would have been possible if the several lines had operated independently or if the plant had been readied for operation for the first time (today)... ."

ebruary 1968 snow dumped several inches on South Louisville (Ky.) yard as switchman and crew worked cut of cars up ladder track at south nd of yard (which was closed when newer Osborn Yard opened in 1977).

Two passengers, assisted by a train attendant, boarded the *Humming Bird* at Louisville on one of its first trips in 1946.

"It's Smart To Travel By Train" 4

On the afternoon of April 30, 1971, L&N's *Pan-American*—and dozens of well known "name" passenger trains of other railroads - departed from their respective termini for the last times. The next day, May 1, new Amtrak streamliners of the National Railroad Passenger Corporation made their bow on 21 intercity and long-distance routes across the nation to end a century-plus era of passenger service on the L&N and most other individual railroads.

On that fateful May 1 in L&N Land, a new daily Chicago-Louisville-Montgomery-to Florida streamliner replaced an every-other-day schedule provided by L&N, SCL, and a Chicago-Louisville connection via Penn **Central**. Cars forming that pre-Amtrak service were handled as part of the consist of the *Pan-American* between Louisville-Montgomery. L&N's only other trains still running in late April, 1972, were a St. Louis-Atlanta remnant of the *Georgian* and a Chicago-Danville commuter run-of-sorts inherited from the C&EI. Neither survived beyond April 30.

While passengers contributed less than 10 percent of L&N's total traffic revenues, the railroad nonetheless operated a rather extensive intercity passenger service during much of its history. Included were the Cincinnati-New Orleans main line trains as well as Midwest-

Pine Knot Special was the name locals gave to the Foley Branch train, which connected that Southern Alabama community with the main line at Bay Minette. Long after most L&N steam power ceased to burn wood as fuel, a dozen or so engines like balloon-stacked 2105, assigned to the south-end of the system, continued to burn wood scraps, available in quantity from area mills and yards. Together with crew and admiring friends, the "Special" paused at Loxley, Al., about 1905.

Florida services, jointly run with connecting railroads via the Atlanta, Cincinnati and Evansville gateways. Between Montgomery-New Orleans, L&N also participated in handling "Crescent Route" (New York-Washington-New Orleans) trains as well as direct New Orleans-Jacksonville trains.

L&N's passenger car fleet embraced the major car types—coaches, baggage and mail, dining and lounge cars, together with sleeping cars provided for most of the pre-Amtrak years by the Pullman Company. In more recent decades, new car purchases added lightweight streamlined equipment to the consist of trains, while company shops at South Louisville upgraded dozens of older cars. Among the traveling public, L&N's dining car fare was well remembered, especially for the fresh Gulf Coast seafood gumbo and the Duncan Hines Kentucky Ham breakfasts.

Early Rail Travel in L&N Land

The very beginnings of L&N passenger service might be traced back to the two previously mentioned railroads, the Lexington & Ohio and the Pontchartrain. Both roads were chartered in 1830, offering a year or so later travel—albeit initially by horse-pulled cars—over their respective routes out of Lexington, Ky., and New Orleans, La. Two other pioneering passenger routes in L&N Land need to be mentioned—the Western & Atlantic's Atlanta-to-Chattanooga line, in operation by 1850, and the Nashville & Chattanooga, offering travelers schedules from 1854 on, between its namesake cities.

Passenger service between Louisville and Nashville began on November 1, 1859. Even before the main line to Nashville was completed, however, the L&N provided a local service of sorts, first from Louisville to Elizabethtown, Ky., then progressively southward to "end of track," with stage coaches conveying passengers around the uncompleted gaps in trackage.

L&N's first public timetable advertised two trains each way making the 185-mile trip in about 9 hours. Then, on the eve of the Civil War in April 1861, through passenger service between Louisville and Memphis was inaugurated. L&N trains from the main line at Bowling Green connected at Guthrie, Ky., with the recently finished Memphis, Clarksville & Louisville, which, in turn, joined the Memphis & Ohio at Paris, Tenn.

Those new rail services offered obvious advantages to travelers in speed, convenience and dependability over competing stage lines and steamboats. The nine-hour Louisville-Nashville schedules were three times faster than those of the stages, which took 27 hours for the one-way trip. Ads in 1861 Memphis newspapers declared that running times to Louisville - about 28 hours over the "new lines" - bettered the best river-packet timing between the two cities by 50 hours!

Of course on-train amenities offered passengers in the 1860s and 70s were spartan. Generous quantities of soot and cinders showered in through open windows, and dining service was virtually non-existent, except for whatever "vittles" the hardy traveler could carry or bolt down at infrequent meal stops. However, sleeping cars were introduced on the L&N as early as 1869, when "Rip Van Winkle" palace sleepers began operating between Louisville, Memphis and New Orleans. In the early 1880s, through service was established between Cincinnati and New Orleans, and two solid main line trains were running straight through, after 1886.

Sleepers to Dixie and Florida

L&N's growth as a major Southeast region carrier in the 1880s and 1890s enabled it to greatly improve its passenger service. In those decades, the railroad introduced long distance trains featuring equipment which gave patrons much more comfort and safety in travel than ever before. "The through-car service of the L&N," proclaimed timetables of the period, "is unsurpassed by any line in the South. Sleepers are the latest model Pullman vestibuled buffet

H. C. Hill/L&N Collection, U of L Archives

For many years, NC&StL operated a 20-mile ferry on the Tennessee River to transfer passengers and freight between Huntsville and Gadsden, AL. At Hobbs Island, northern terminus of the ferry, G-class Ten-Wheeler 170 prepared to depart with the Huntsville-bound passenger run in December 1920. Steamer Guntersville then landed five freight cars also brought downriver from Guntersville, Al., southern terminus.

cars, and coaches are equipped with all modern improvements."

With completion of the Henderson bridge across the Ohio River in 1885 and standardization of track gauges in 1886, the L&N launched a St. Louis-Nashville sleeping-car line. That was followed in 1892 by a Nashville-Jacksonville, Fl., through sleeper promoted by Major W. L. Danley, NC&StL's general passenger agent, as the *Dixie Flyer*. A companion Nashville-Atlanta sleeper, also moving over the NC&StL, became the *Quickstep*.

Success of those services as well as the Florida resort boom led to a long-distance winter-season train, launched by the L&N, NC&StL and C&EI in December, 1901. Called the *Chicago & Florida Limited*, this train became the first of a succession of elegantly equipped and appointed "named" trains to link the Midwest with the beaches and resorts in the Sunshine State and along the Alabama and Mississippi Gulf Coast.

Increased Florida travel also spurred L&N, with ACL, C&EI, CofG and NC&StL, to begin year-round operations between Chicago and Florida in 1908. The *Dixie Flyer* sleeper car run was transformed into a solid train which begin running daily between Chicago-Jacksonville. In the meantime, completion of the Etowah, Tenn.-Cartersville, Ga. segment of L&N's so-called "east side" main line led to improved Midwest-Florida travel via Cincinnati. The *South Atlantic Flyer*, offering direct service between the Queen City and Jacksonville, was inaugurated in 1909. A Louisville section joined the main train at Corbin, Ky. Renamed the *Southland* in 1915, the train also forwarded through Pullmans between Great Lakes and Michigan cities and Florida.

On the Cincinnati-New Orleans main line, the *New Orleans Limited* became the premiere train, by 1910 offering a two-nights- out schedule. With the 1900s also came heavier steel coaches and Pullmans, steam vapor heating, electric lights, lounge and meal service. The first three dining cars went into service on main line trains in 1901, L&N's dining car department and commissary also having been formed that year.

New Train for The Jazz Decade

The zenith of passenger service on America's railroads was reached in the 1920s. Rail travel was "it" in the jazz decade, and more people rode the crack expresses and limiteds than ever before, or since. In 1921, over one billion passengers were carried by American railroads, a record which has never been surpassed. L&N's top passenger year was 1920, during which more than 17 million passengers rode its trains. Even so, in that busy, hectic decade, L&N as well as other lines felt the pinch from growing auto, bus and air competition. The "passenger problem" appeared on the pages of employee and industry trade publications with more frequency. Articles in the *L&N Magazine* encouraged employees to "talk up our trains" to get more folks to travel by rail. During the 1920s, the L&N purchased a vast fleet of steel equipment. With the exception of locals and branch line runs, all main line passenger trains were assigned modern steel cars.

The L&N's most celebrated train, *The Pan-American*, was born on December 5, 1921. Operating on a daily one-night out schedule between Cincinnati and New Orleans, the *Pan*, as the train came to be known across the South, was an immediate success. Through cars between Cincinnati-Memphis were handled south of Bowling Green, Ky., by a Memphis Line section, running via Clarksville and Paris, Tenn.. Then in May, 1925, the Pan became an all-Pullman train, with new cars delivered especially for its consist and powerful new locomotives (which arrived in 1926) to speed it over the hillier divisions of the railroad.

Ron Flanary Collection

Train 92, the St. Louis section of the *Dixie Limited*, approached East St. Louis in a winter scene from the early 1940s. Most of the "Dixie" route trains via Evansville offered connections to St. Louis via this route. K4B 260 was on the business end of No. 92 that day.

Behind K-5 Pacific 267, the nine-car all-Pullman *Pan-American* headed south from Louisville in this promotional view from summer 1925. An artist's air brush added hints of speed! All-Pullman until the early 1930s, the *Pan* added a combine and coach in the Great Depression but still treated Pullman patrons to its "radio-observation car."

The re-equipped *Pan* consisted of brand new 12 section-drawing room Pullman sleeping cars, new 36-seat dining cars with mahogany decor, baggage-club library cars, and at the rear, 20-seat drawing room parlor-observation cars, with valet service. There, passengers could enjoy their favorite radio programs, which they listened to through individual headsets. A 26-seat parlor car operated between Cincinnati and Memphis. Other improvement to the *Pan* were made consistently, and during the early 1930s, the parlor observation cars were replaced by bedroom observation cars. The train was also air-conditioned.

In 1933, the *Pan* became a radio celebrity. Each afternoon, its passage was broadcast by WSM Radio in Nashville. A track-side microphone positioned just south of the city at Brentwood, Tn., (later moved to Vine Hill Tower) picked up the whistle and sounds of the speeding train as it highballed south. WSM announcers also gave the name of the *Pan's* engineer each day, and later, on anniversaries of the startup of the broadcasts, special programming originated from the train itself. World War II and diesels curtailed the shows in

1945, but, thanks to such exposure, the *Pan* won for herself and her railroad a host of friends in many states.

Running on a slightly slower schedule between Cincinnati and New Orleans, the *New Orleans Limited* (Trains No. 1 and 4) was the companion train to the *Pan* and offered coach, dining and sleeping car services. The *Limited* was renamed the *"Azalean"* in 1936. Through Chicago- Mobile Pullmans and coaches were also handled by Nos. 1-4 south of Nashville. Those cars moved on the *"Dixie Limited"* via Evansville (or north of Nashville). Trains No. 7-8, for some years known as the *"Eastern Express"* (later the *Atlantic Flyer*), operated between Cincinnati, Louisville, Nashville and Birmingham, carrying through New York-Louisville and Nashville Pullmans (which Pennsy worked, north of Cincinnati).

Dixie-to-Florida Upgrades

The *Dixie Limited*, first inaugurated in 1913 as a seasonal train, became by the 1920s the year-round mate to the more famous *Dixie Flyer* on the ACL-C&EI-CofG-L&N-NC&StL "Dixie Route." The *Limited* offered afternoon

Train 15, the *South Wind*, departed Union Station, Louisville, in May 1941 behind K-5 275. The six-wheeled roller bearing tender, originally built for K-7 experimental Pacific 295, trailed the 275 while South Louisville corrected 295's engine truck bearing problem. With a 27-1/2 ton capacity, the big tender enabled the *Wind* to run without picking up coal between Louisville-Montgomery 490 miles.

departure from Chicago, with next morning arrival in Atlanta and a second morning termination in South Florida cities. Even faster service was offered in 1936, with inauguration of the seasonal *Dixieland*, making the Chicago— Miami run in just over 32 hours and with only one night out. Meanwhile, on the Chicago-Louisville-Montgomery-Florida route, another seasonal train, the *Florida Arrow,* was launched in January 1935 and ran many winters until 1949.

Between Cincinnati, Knoxville, Atlanta and Jacksonville, the *Flamingo* (first trips 1925) joined the *Southland* to provide companion service. Overnight Pullman lines between Louisville, Knoxville and Atlanta were part of the *Flamingo's* consist and were handled by trains No. 21-24 over the Lebanon Branch (Louisville-Corbin). Even some local trains picked up informal names, such as the *Hook and Eye* local which plied between Atlanta and Knoxville via the "old line", and the *Bluegrass*

Locals, trains No. 15-20, on the Louisville-Frankfort-Lexington line. For the latter trains, Lexington served as the transfer point to day trains to and from Hazard and Eastern Kentucky. Corbin became the junction for passengers connecting between main line Cincy-Atlanta trains, the Lebanon Branch runs, and locals working the Cumberland Valley branch to Harlan, Middlesboro, Lynch and Norton, Va.

L&N also helped move another famous train, the *Crescent Limited*, over a portion of its New York- New Orleans run. Interestingly, a predecessor service which dated back to the early 1900s offered through cars on a coast-to-coast schedule via the Crescent City. In time, that service evolved into a solid Washington-New Orleans train, with L&N participating, between Montgomery, Mobile and New Orleans. Beginning in 1926, that train was renamed the *Crescent Limited* and re-equipped with an all—Pullman consist (excepting dining and head-end cars).

In May 1941, L-1 407 has No. 98, the northbound *Pan-American*, in tow just south of Louisville. The visible portion of the train included two baggage cars, two coaches, a diner, and three Pullmans. Longer consists in the late 1930s mandated that L-1 Mountain type engines work Nos. 98-99 over the hillier Cincy and Louisville Divisions north of Nashville.

While primarily a Southern Railway venture, Nos. 37-38 received good handling from the L&N and the two West Point Route roads on their part of the operation (Atlanta-Montgomery). The train was not streamlined until 1949, at which time the L&N participated more fully in purchase of new lightweight equipment. A sister train, the *Piedmont Limited*, was also worked by L&N and the West Point Route south of Atlanta.

Airplanes, automobiles, intercity and regional busses continued to slice off more of L&N's share of the passenger "pie" during the late 1920s and Depression-era 1930s. Across the system, dozens of locals, secondary route and branch line trains were either discontinued outright or operated less frequently. On some branches, a "mixed train" service was substituted for the previously all-passenger runs. Although only a few new cars were bought during the decade, L&N modernized a number of coaches used on the *Pan* and *Azalean*. It also slashed fares and offered travel bargains to attract more ridership

Age of Streamliners

The age of the lightweight streamliners dawned in L&N Land in December, 1940, with the inauguration of three Midwest-Florida all-coach speedsters, the *Dixie Flagler*, *South*

Wind and *City of Miami*. L&N participated in the coordinated operation of two of the trains, the *Flagler* and *Wind*; the *City* ran over IC, CofG, ACL, and FEC rails, via Birmingham and Columbus, Ga.

In a splendid action photo from winter 1949-50, mainline local No. 7 rolled through the Kentucky countryside south of Elizabethtown. The train's L-1 Mountain left a snow-white exhaust plume to mark its passing.

On December 17th, the *Dixie Flagler* departed Chicago on its run to Florida over the C&EI to Evansville, L&N to Nashville and NC&StL there to Atlanta; the Atlanta, Birmingham and Coast (AB&C) forwarded the *Flagler*

to Waycross, Ga., where ACL took over to Jacksonville; Florida East Coast (FEC), which owned the seven-car train, operated the final leg to Miami. Four of the participating roads—C&EI, L&N, NC&StL and AB&C—dolled up 4-6-2 Pacific-type locomotives for the Flagler service. L&N streamlined its K-5 heavy Pacific 277 for the Evansville-Nashville sprint, while NC&StL outfitted its 536 in similar decor. The IC-CofG *City of Miami*, which made its debut trip from the Windy City on December 18th, was pulled by an EMD single unit E6 passenger diesel.

Then, on December 19th, the *South Wind*, third of the three streamliners in the pool service, steamed south from Chicago to Louisville over rails of the Pennsylvania Railroad The *Wind's* seven-car tuscan red consist was owned by the Pennsy, which had streamlined a K4s 4-6-2 for the run. At Louisville, L&N's black and silver- shrouded 295 coupled on to forward the *Wind* to Nashville and Montgomery. There, an ACL P-5 class 4-6-2, took over to Jacksonville, with FEC working the consist on to Miami.

The L&N served as the intermediate carrier for the *Flagler* and *Wind* trains over two different routes, which intersected at Nashville. All three trains were fast, very fast indeed, covering overall Chicago- Miami schedules in 29 hours, 30 minutes. Just two hours, 15 minutes were allowed for layovers at Miami, with 10 hours, 45 minutes given to turn and service equipment at Chicago. Uniform consists for the trains included a baggage-coach, four reclining seat coaches, a full diner and an observation—lounge car. The three coach

L&N Collection, U of L Archives

On this summer 1944 day, "lst 99," was not the *Pan-American* but, rather, J-4 1875 barreling south from Louisville with a solid string of Pennsy P70 coaches carrying the military. Flags on the troop section indicated mainline *Pan* or following section was close behind.

streamliners provided daily service between Chicago and Miami, but while they were intended only for seasonal operation, they became so well patronized that the participating railroads decided to run them year-round. That pattern continued throughout the World War II years (1941-1945) and until the late 1940s.

Serving The War Effort

Above and beyond the call of duty … How better to cite the role played by the L&N, NC&StL, C&EI and sister carriers in transporting unprecedented numbers of military and civilian passengers during World War II? In 1939, L&N trains carried some 3.2 million passengers; by 1944, the road's passenger traffic volume had swollen to 12.4 million travelers. Extra cars on regular trains, frequent second sections and "Extras" or "Mains" helped move

troops and other travelers. More seats and tables were added in dining cars to increase their capacities. A February, 1944 issue of RAILWAY AGE noted that the L&N served 2,380,547 meals in its 29 dining cars during the previous year. Half of those meals were served to uniformed military personnel. An additional 816,230 passengers were served at their seats by waiters providing sandwiches, coffee and milk. The AGE article also observed that L&N's dining car department showed a profit for the first time in its 42 years of existence, thanks to the record wartime travel!

Maximum utilization was made of all passenger equipment and motive power, and because of overwhelming demand on sleeping cars during late 1944-5, the L&N, as did many other railroads, discontinued Pullman lines of less than 450 miles. Aged open-platform wooden coaches were also pressed into use

W. B. Thurman

Not far behind No. 7 and on the same winter day as the photo on page 72, Tuscan red K-7 295 hit her stride between Louisville and Nashville on train 15, the *South Wind*. L&N repainted the big Pacific tuscan red in the late 1940s to match equipment of the Pennsy-owned Chicago-Florida coach streamliner, which made its first run on December 19, 1940.

on some local trains operating in and out of Louisville during that time. Badly needed motive power, meanwhile, was received in spring and summer 1942 with delivery of 16 EMD 2,000 h.p. E6 diesel units, which immediately went into service to wheel *Pan-Americans*, *Southlands* and *Dixie Limiteds* lengthened far beyond their normal consists by war travel. The tireless efforts over long hours by train and dining-car crews, porters, station agents and operators and hosts of other employees helped heighten the L&N's great contribution in support of America's war effort.

Georgians, Humming Birds Take Flight

The immediate post-World War II years brought more streamliners to L&N Land as Old Reliable continued its program of upgrading passenger services. Two routes—Cincinnati to New Orleans and St. Louis to Atlanta—were selected by the passenger department to receive new trains; the main line was already well served by the flagship *Pan-American* and companion *Azalean*, operating on comfortable if only moderately fast schedules. Faster day streamliners, felt traffic men, might well attract more ridership between cities served by L&N's

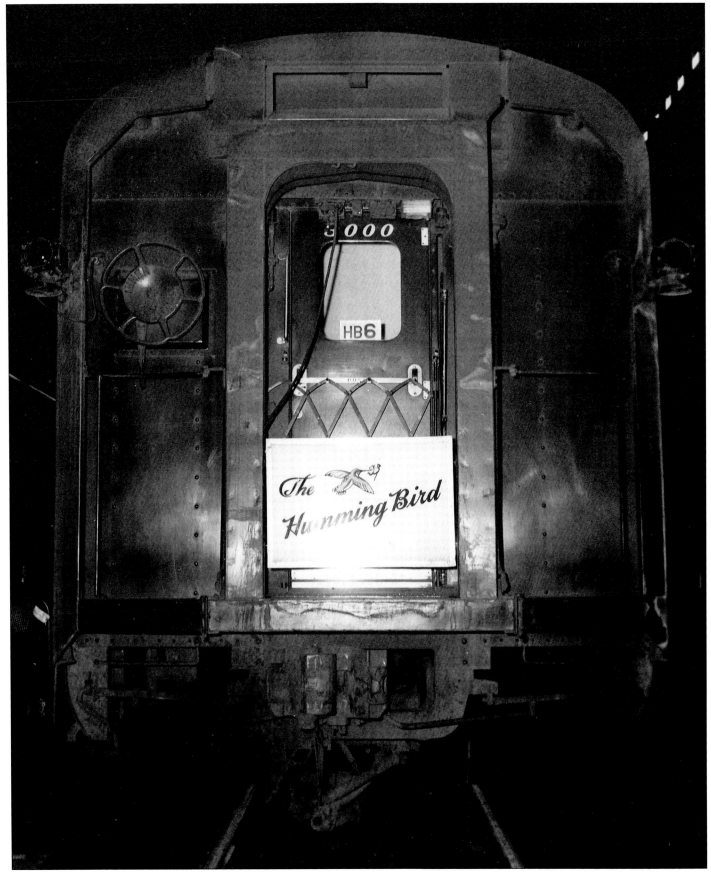

Tavern-lounge 3000 *Churchill Downs* displayed the *Humming Bird's* markers and tail sign. What with picking up and dropping cars at various intermediate points, later practice called for the train not to be so identified.

A staged publicity photo had "passengers" being served by a white-jacketed attendant aboard tavern-lounge car *Carnival Club,* part of the consist of the *Humming Bird*

main lines. Traditionally, St. Louis-Atlanta formed part of the Midwest-Florida "Dixie Route;" prospects for all-coach daylight runs over that route were also considered good.

During spring 1946, the company announced plans to place in service two new all-coach lightweight streamliners for the coming fall. Twenty coaches and eight diners and tavern-lounge cars (making up four train-sets) were ordered by the L&N and NC&StL from American Car and Foundry. Each train-set consisted of seven cars, including five coaches, one diner, and one tavern-lounge car (the all-coach consists were "aimed" at an "economy" market). A contest was held to pick names for the new trains. Almost 300,000 people entered the contest, and in September 1946, the L&N announced the winning names: *Humming Bird* for the mainline Cincy-Gulf Coast train and the *Georgian* for the St. Louis-Atlanta train, which the NC&StL would move south of Nashville.

Trimmed in dark blue and silver, the new all-coach liners were as comfortable inside as they were striking to look at outside. Coaches seated 60 passengers (except for one 48-seat chair-lounge coach in each consist). Individual reclining and revolving seats took advantage of full vision five-foot windows. Coaches also had individually controlled fluorescent lighting at each seat, recessed in the lower portion of overhead luggage racks. Overall car lighting was provided by recessed ceiling fixtures beaming down directly on the aisles. Spacious lounges for men and women with stainless steel-encased twin lavatories were situated at each end of the cars.

Dining cars seated 48 passengers at 12 tables adjacent to the wide windows. Full length mirrors were placed in partitions at each end of dining areas. Varying shades of reds and browns alternated with fawn colored upholstery; dark maroon carpeting and ivory walls and ceilings enhanced the color schemes of each car.

The tavern-lounge car interiors were divided by glass partitions into two sections with sofas and deep lounge chairs. The lounge section provided seating for 28 passengers, while the tavern section seated 24, some at tables and others at leather upholstered horseshoe-shaped seats. The two areas were separated by a curved bar. Restrooms were found at the tavern end of the cars, together with lockers and the conductor's office, which housed the train loud speaker system controls.

To power the new trains, L&N assigned new EMD 2,000 h.p. E7 passenger diesels, eight having been delivered a year before (1945) in anticipation of the streamliners. The E7s wore a blue-silver livery to match the stainless steel equipment, and initially, one unit was assigned per train. Units protecting the joint L&N-NC&StL *Georgian* carried a modified nose emblem with initials of both roads.

Delivered in late October 1946, the trains toured the L&N and NC&StL systems, standing on display for several days at major cities.

L&N Collection, UofL Archives

The brand-new *Humming Bird* posed for publicity photos at the Baxter Avenue station, Louisville, in November 1946 just before entering service on the Cincinnati-New Orleans run. Blue and silver E7 459A led a seven-car consist of new American Car & Foundry lightweight cars.

Nashvillians were treated to simultaneous displays of the *Georgian* and *Humming Bird*, spotted on adjacent tracks at Union Station. Then, on November 17, the new streamliners went into daily service over their respective routes; they became America's first post-World War II streamliners.

Steam Streamliner For Memphis

Just six months after the *Georgian* and *Humming Bird* were inaugurated, the NC&StL made a remarkable bid to improve passenger service between Nashville and Memphis with a new six-car dayliner, the *City Of Memphis*. The road jumped ahead of many larger systems then awaiting new equipment by transforming old Pullmans into streamlined cars for its new service. The West Nashville Shops did the work, giving the cars new roller-bearing trucks, air—conditioning and new interior configurations at a cost of about $350,000, much less than commercial car builders. The consist included a baggage-RPO, three coaches, a diner-lounge and a flat-end observation-coach-lounge car. NC&StL later rebuilt several other cars as lightweight coaches to add to the *City* on travel—heavy weekends and holidays.

To power the *City*, NC&StL stuck with steam, rebuilding a 1913 Baldwin heavy Pacific-type with cast cylinders and forward frame section, roller bearings, six-wheel tender and a blue-gray-black shroud to cover boiler, stack and domes. Launched in mid-May 1947, the dayliner made the 478-mile roundtrip from Memphis to Nashville and back. Five-hour run-

H. C. Hill/L&N Collection, U of L Archives
A World War II version of the *Dixie Flyer,* northward Train 94, paused on the curve at the foot of Lookout Mountain, just west of Chattanooga. A two-year old J-3 4-8-4 headed the war-swollen first secion on that July 1944 day.

J. Parker Lamb

The southbound *Azalean,* Train 1, slipped out of Montgomery behind E6s 751 and 774. The consist on that June 1955 day included six baggage cars, three coaches and a single Pullman. By then, Nos. 1-4 played second fiddle to the faster *Humming Bird* and *Pan-American.* The Alabama River and the historic Union Station train shed were visible in the background.

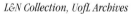

L&N Collection, UofL Archives

L&N's one-of-a-kind railcar, gas-electric no. 3600, worked NF&S Branch schedules for some years between Columbia, Tenn., and Florence, Ala. The car, at Columbia about 1940 with a wood baggage in tow, was then painted olive green to match conventional passenger equipment, and in typical steam power fashion, its number was affixed on the headlight lens.

Nicely matched C&EI EMD E7s brought the northbound *Humming Bird* into Chicago sometime during 1951. For several years, the *Bird* and companion *Georgian* ran as separate trains between Nashville and Chicago, so heavy was their patronage.

ning times for each one-way leg were scheduled, with nine intermediate stops. One of NC&StL's wartime dual service 4-8-4s replaced the Pacific in 1949 when it was retired. The 4-8-4, in turn, gave way to a boiler-equipped passenger GP7, when the road dieselized in 1952-3.

L&N's own two all-coach streamliners, meanwhile, were not entirely successful in their intended service. Ridership, especially on the *Georgian* (Nos. 80-81), did not match earlier predictions; passenger department studies indicated that the Chicago-Atlanta corridor (rather than St. Louis-Atlanta) was much the stronger market, and in midyear 1948, the *Georgian* was shifted to a C&EI-L&N-NC&StL route on an overnight schedule, complete with sleepers (initially, heavyweight Pullmans) and a St. Louis connection. Late afternoon departures were scheduled at Chicago and Atlanta, with next morning arrivals at the opposite termini. Thus, the stage was set for what became one of the L&N's most heavily patronized trains.

While remaining a Cincinnati-New Orleans train, the *Humming Bird* (Nos. 5-6) in September 1948 received sleeping car accomodations in the form of a 12-section heavyweight Pullman (which also satisfied previous complaints about lack of such accommodations). As with the *Georgian* cars, the *Bird's* sleepers were repainted blue and silver, with "shadowlining" in the below-window silver panels to simulate the aluminum fluting contained on the new ACF cars. Heavyweight L&N diner 2712 was similarly redecorated.

More fine tuning of the *Georgian-Bird* streamliners in the months ahead led to significant schedule changes, resulting in advantageous service coordinations for both trains at Nashville. Departure of the southbound *Bird* from Cincinnati was delayed from afternoon to early evening, so that at Nashville, both the *Bird* and *Georgian* could interchange cars. A Cincinnati-Atlanta sleeper, for example, was switched from No. 5 to No. 81, while several through sleepers from Chicago to deep South/Gulf Coast cities (previously handled on No. 1, the southbound *Azalean*) were dropped by the Georgian and added to the *Bird's* consist. Northward, the two trains pulled off a similar "Nashville shuffle," as the late Frank E.

L&N Collection, UofL Archives

On April 20, 1951, spanking new GP7 500 made its first run on train 23, the Louisville-Corbin day passenger local via the Lebanon Branch. Night-time trains on the same route handled through Louisville-Atlanta Pullmans, which the *Flamingo* Nos. 17-18 moved south of Corbin.

Shaffer, author and TRAINS associate editor, nicknamed the midnight car-swap in the Music city. Gulf-to-Chicago and St. Louis through cars were left by No. 6 and added to No. 80's consist. The Atlanta-Cincy cars, meantime, came off No. 80 and were coupled to the rear of No. 6. And so forth.

By 1951, traffic had grown to such levels that a separate section of the *Humming Bird* was established between Chicago and Nashville, the train running as No. 93 south-bound and No. 54 northbound. The *Bird's* Chicago section was scheduled about 15 to 30 minutes behind the *Georgian* in both directions. The revised schedules of the *Bird* also precipitated improvement that year in overnight Cincinnati-Louisville-Memphis service. A Pullman and through coach formerly handled southward on the *Azalean* between Cincy and Bowling Green were added to the *Bird's* consist in the early 1950s, and a similar upgrading for northward Memphis—Cincinnati

H. C. Hill/L&N Collection, UofL Archives

The *City of Memphis*, train 6 between Nashville and Memphis, descended McEwen Hill in Western Tennessee in 1947 with streamlined Pacific 535 and six streamlined cars, rebuilt from old Pullmans. Running on fastest schedules ever beteem the two cities, the dayliner still failed to stem the postwar automotive tide, and it shrank to a nameless two-car local by discontinuance time, September 2, 1958.

R. D. Sharpless/Frank E. Ardrey, Jr. Collection

An August 1953 view of the *Southland* showed it northbound through Vinings, Ga., on NC&StL rails. Consists of the heavyweight Midwest-Florida train often contained a colorful mix of L&N, ACL and FEC passenger equipment.

cars was accomplished several years later. The *Pan-American*, incidentally, had long offered through car service to and from the Memphis Line for daytime travel.

New Cars For the Streamliner Fleet

In 1953, delivery of 29 lightweight sleeping cars from Pullman enabled the L&N, with C&EI and NC&StL, to replace older heavyweight cars on the Bird and Georgian as well as on the Pan-American. Cars were the attractive, well remembered *Pine* series, each bearing the name of a pine tree species found in the Southern U.S. With a "6-6-4" configuration (six roomettes, six open sections and four double-bedrooms), the *Pine* cars were painted a dark blue, with gray roofs, black trucks and imitation gold script lettering.

It should be noted that, earlier in the post-

war period, L&N had already upgraded several of the sleeping car lines for the *Pan-American* when it purchased several all-room "River" series 10-roomette, 6-double bedroom cars from Pullman. Among lines improved were Nashville- and Louisville-New York overnight sleepers, which the Pennsy handled north of Cincinnati. In 1955, 13 new ACF-built lightweight 60-seat coaches costing $1.8 million, also joined L&N's passenger car fleet, going into *Bird/Georgian* consists. The cars featured leather reclining seats and murals of L&N Land scenes on end-walls. Original cars from *Bird/Georgian* consists were then shifted to the *Pan* and other trains.

The post-World War II period was one of optimism and unprecedented demand for peace-time travel. To meet that demand, railroads purchased passenger equipment in rela-

continued on page 92

American Car & Foundry delivered 13 new 60-passenger, center-partition streamlined coaches in 1955. Before being assigned to the *Humming Bird*, the first car was displayed under the Louisville Union Station train shed. Interior arrangement for cars is shown below.

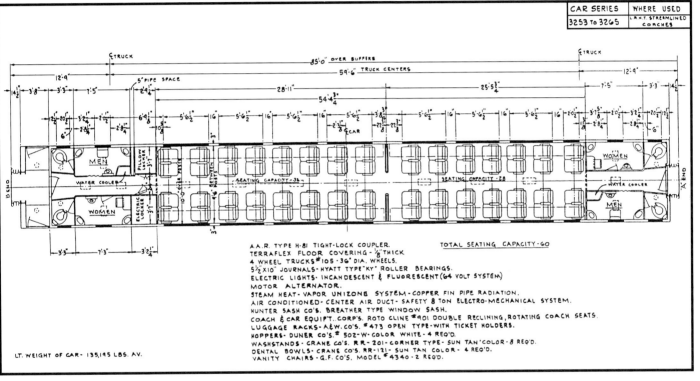

CAR SERIES	WHERE USED
3253 To 3265	L.&N.T. STREAMLINED COACHES

A.A.R. TYPE H-81 TIGHT-LOCK COUPLER.
TERRAFLEX FLOOR COVERING - ⅛ THICK
4 WHEEL TRUCKS #105 - 36" DIA. WHEELS.
5½ X10" JOURNALS - HYATT TYPE "KY" ROLLER BEARINGS.
ELECTRIC LIGHTS - INCANDESCENT & FLUORESCENT (64 VOLT SYSTEM)
MOTOR ALTERNATOR.
STEAM HEAT - VAPOR UNIZONE SYSTEM - COPPER FIN PIPE RADIATION.
AIR CONDITIONED - CENTER AIR DUCT - SAFETY 8 TON ELECTRO-MECHANICAL SYSTEM.
HUNTER SASH CO'S. BREATHER TYPE WINDOW SASH.
COACH & CAR EQUIP'T. CORP'S. ROTO CLINE #901 DOUBLE RECLINING, ROTATING COACH SEATS.
LUGGAGE RACKS - A&W CO'S. #473 OPEN TYPE - WITH TICKET HOLDERS.
HOPPERS - DUNER CO'S. # 502-W- COLOR WHITE - 4 REQ'D.
WASHSTANDS - CRANE CO'S. RR-201- CORNER TYPE - SUN TAN COLOR - 8 REQ'D.
DENTAL BOWLS - CRANE CO'S. RR-121- SUN TAN COLOR - 4 REQ'D.
VANITY CHAIRS - G.F. CO'S. MODEL # 4340 - 2 REQ'D.

TOTAL SEATING CAPACITY - 60

LT. WEIGHT OF CAR - 135,195 LBS. AV.

Heavyweight 36-seat diner 2712 was one of several older cars which received a "shadowline" paint job to match streamlined ACF-built cars for the *Georgian/Humming Bird.* The blue and silver car was at South Louisville in January 1950.

ACF-built in 1929, 36-seat diner 2725 in its original olive-gold lettering scheme served famous L&N meals on mainline trains. Years later, the car ran on the *Georgian* between Atlanta and Chicago, or until the late 1960s. Several L&N diners bore names of famous hostelries and restaurants in the south.

This is the interior of diner-lounge 2800, *Dixie Traveler,* a former C&EI car which in 1959 replaced the full diner and tavern-lounge on the *Pan-American* between Cincinnati and Montgomery. Car and its sister were modified in the mid-1960s with lengthwise counters and seats replacing tables.

Royal Canal and *Royal Street* were L&N's twin solarium-lounge/bedroom cars assigned to the *Crescent.* One of the pair was displayed at New Orleans with the train in 1954 when the new Union Passenger Terminal opened.

Reclining seats, overhead indirect lighting and full windows enhanced new 60-seat coaches on the new post-World War II *Georgian* and *Humming Bird* streamliners. Four additional coaches had 48 seats, lounge section for 11 persons. Seating arrangements and floor plans for full coaches, dining cars and tavern-lounge cars are shown below and on opposite page.

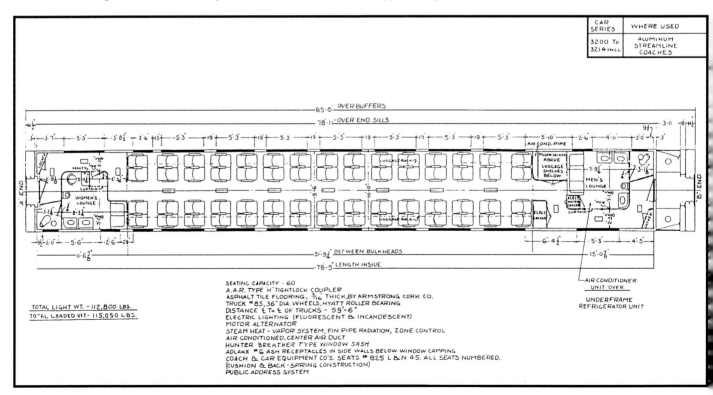

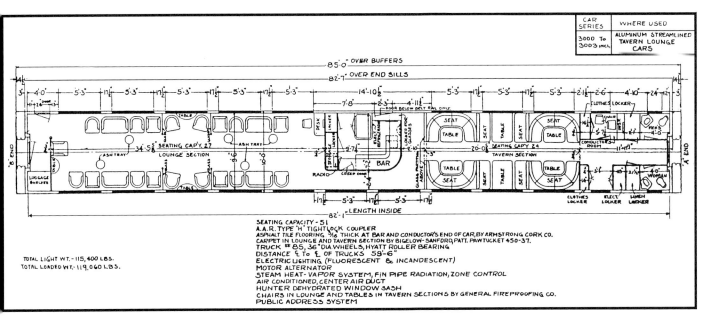

L&N Collection, U of L Archives

Tavern-Lounge No. 3000, *Boston Club,* at Louisville in the mid-1950s, was turned out by ACF in 1946 as part of four seven-car trainsets for the then-new *Georgian* and *Humming Bird* streamliners. First named *Churchill Downs,* the car was renamed in 1952 and ran for some years in the consist of the *Bird.*

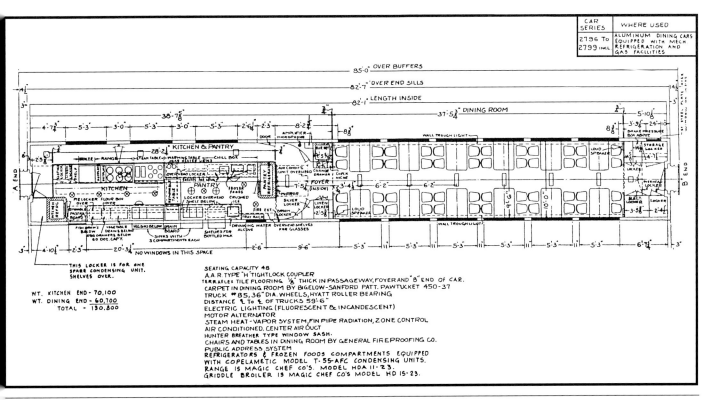

In the 1960s, L&N adopted a green-and-white paint plan for stations in smaller communities like Barbourville, Ky on the Cumberland Valley Division. With little or no passenger service on many routes, such buildings often housed offices and storage space for signal maintainers and other MofW forces.

At several division and junction points, notably Corbin and Ravenna, both in Kentucky, and at Etowah and Paris, in Tennessee, stations shared space with divisional offices. The rambling Etowah station for some years housed dispatchers and other operating staff for the old Knoxville & Atlanta Division. Restored in L&N's familiar olive-and-white scheme, Etowah hosted a weekend of excursion trips to Copperhill and the Hiwassee Loop in October 1986.

Bob Bell, Jr.

Opened in 1900, the beautiful Nashville Union Station served trains of L&N, NC&StL and Amtrak. In March 1965, the northbound *Pan-American* behind an E6/E8/E6 trio, loaded passengers, mail and express for Louisville and beyond.

L&N also contributed several lightweight stainless steel coaches for the *Crescent*. The 52-seat 3250 was at South Louisville Shops for repairs in 1963.

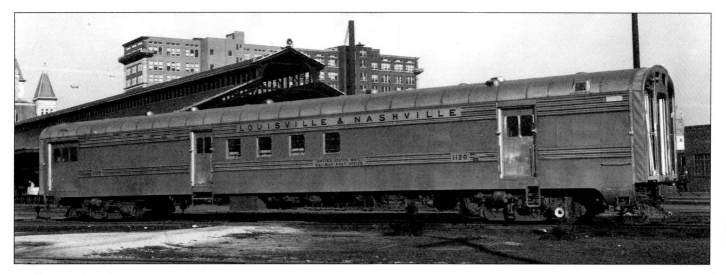

Two stainless steel 81-foot long baggage/RPO cars were built by Pullman-Standard in 1949 for the *Crescent* pool of cars. The 1120, at Louisville just after entering service, was later renumbered to 1550 and converted to a full-length baggage car.

L&N Collection/UofL Archives

Above: Fresh from its conversion at South Louisville, Reclining seat coach 2561 was displayed downtown at Union Station in 1948. L&N began painting passenger equipment dark blue with gold script lettering just after World War II, replacing the earlier dark olive green scheme and its gold Roman lettering.

L&N Collection, U of L Archives

Right: Many thoroughbreds also rode to and from Louisville by rail. Aboard an L&N baggage car outfitted for horse transport, 1955 Kentucky Derby challenger *Nashua* nibbled hay from his handler.

tively large quantities and extensively rebuilt older equipment to like-new conditions. Interstate Commerce Commission figures show that, between 1945-1958, U.S. lines and the Pullman Company spent more than $1.3 billion for new passenger cars and motive power. Further, the postwar bid with new trains was matched by faster schedules, attractive reduced-fare schemes, frequent advertising, new stations and many other innovations. Total expenditures for these improvements - including the new equipment and power - were borne entirely by the railroads themselves.

The *Crescent*, which L&N handled between Montgomery and New Orleans, was also upgraded in the post-war years. In 1949, owner Southern Railway ordered some 141 new stainless steel lightweight cars for the *Crescent*, *Piedmont* and other named trains. Joining the participating roads, L&N contributed three coaches, five roomette-bedroom sleepers, two bedroom observation lounge cars, two RPO cars and two baggage-dormitory units for the trains' equipment pool. Also in 1949, the fast new *Gulf Wind* made its debut on the Jacksonville-Pensacola-Mobile-New Orleans route. Together, L&N and Seaboard participated to improve that cross-Florida-Gulf rail link. Overnight schedules were shortened by about five hours by the new trains, their consists including new lightweight sleepers as well upgraded heavyweight coaches, diners and lounges.

During 1949, improvements were also made to the Midwest—Florida streamliner services with the addition of Pullmans to both the *Dixie Flagler* (C&EI-L&N-NC&StL-ACL-FEC route) and the *South Wind* (the Pennsy, L&N-ACL-FEC trains, via Louisville and Montgomery). Previously, the participating roads had added winter—season trains equipped with heavyweight sleepers, diners, et al, to augment the all-coach streamliners. But, after '49, the *Flagler* and *Wind*, with expanded consists and diesels, began operating two out of three days and, eventually, every other day. For the 1954-55 season, the *Flagler* was renamed the *Dixieland* and ran until withdrawn in late 1957. L&N and NC&StL joined C&EI in purchasing new all-room sleepers for the train. Beginning with the Winter 1959-60 season, leased dome-sleepers from the Northern Pacific's North Coast Limited appeared in consists of the *South Wind*, later becoming part of that train's winter consist. The *Wind*, of course, remained in service until 1971, continuing after that as an Amtrak train and eventually renamed the *Floridian*.

J. Parker Lamb

FP7 655 waited in the clear with a local freight at Mississippi City in July 1957, for a fast-stepping troop train behind E6s. The local's head brakeman stood ready to perform a "roll-by" of the passenger extra.

A summary

Principal L&N and NC&StL passenger services as of the early 1950s and from then contemporary timetables:

Cincinnati- New Orleans Mainline

Nos. 1-4, the *Azalean*, Cincinnati- New Orleans-Pullmans, reclining seat coaches, dining car (New Orleans—Birmingham, Louisville-Cincinnati); By the early '50s, Nos. 1-4 had lost sleepers to the *Humming Bird* and were downgraded to mail—express or "head end" trains, making many more local stops. In 1959, Nos. 1-4's southern terminus was shifted to Montgomery.

Nos. 2-3, Cincinnati-Montgomery trains, by 1950s downgraded to head-end, local trains but continuing to handle overnight Cincinnati-Nashville Pullman, also providing day service, Nashville-Montgomery, via former "N&D" route via Columbia, Tn.There, connections were made with Nashville, Florence & Sheffield (NF&S) Branch trains Nos. 11-2 to, from Florence, Ala. For some years, L&N's Brill-built diesel-powered railcar protected the NF&S Branch schedules.

Nos. 5-6, the *Humming Bird*, also Cincinnati-New Orleans streamlined, with Pullmans, reclining seat coaches, dining and tavern-lounge cars, handling Chicago and St. Louis to Montgomery and Mobile through Pullmans, coaches below Nashville, also Memphis-Cincinnati through cars north of Bowling Green.

Nos. 7-8, Cincinnati-Birmingham trains, with No. 8 forwarding Nashville and Louisville-to-New York cars north to Cincinnati for the Pennsy. Dining car, Louisville-Cincinnati. Overnight locals, via "N&D" route and Columbia, between Nashville-Birmingham.

Nos. 15-16, the *South Wind*, every other day Chicago-Florida reserved seat coach-Pullman streamliners (see above), handled by L&N between Louisville-Montgomery.

Nos. 33-34, the *Piedmont Limited*, Montgomery-New Orleans trains (to-from Atlanta and Washington via Southern, West Point Route); Pullmans and coaches, by the mid-1950s, combined with No. 99 south of Montgomery.

Nos. 37-38, the *Crescent*, also Montgomery-New Orleans and from Atlanta, Washington and New York, via West Point route, SR and PRR). Streamlined after 1949, with all-room Pullmans, dining and lounge cars, reclining seat coaches, later combined with No. 98, New Orleans-Montgomery.

Nos. 98-99, *The Pan-American*, Cincinnati-New Orleans trains, with all-room Pullmans, reclining seat coaches, tavern-lounge and dining cars (Cincinnati-Montgomery only). Through cars to and from Memphis Line section handled via Bowling Green, Ky.

Nos. 1-4, 2-3, 5-6, 7-8, and 98-99 provided a combination of intercity express and intrastate services between Cincinnati, Louisville, Nashville, Birmingham and Montgomery. Thus, passengers had a choice of four trains daily in each direction between Cincinnati and Birmingham, and three beyond to Montgomery. Passengers also took advantage of the every-second day *South Wind* (Nos. 15-16) for Louisville-Montgomery corridor travel.

Between Montgomery and New Orleans, the L&N hosted more name trains than on any other line segment. Five were daily trains in each direction, including the *Pan-American*, *Humming Bird* and *Azalean* as well as the *Crescent* and *Piedmont Limited* For a time, a pair of long distance locals also traversed the line. At Flomaton, *Gulf Wind* equipment to and from Jacksonville and Pensacola was added to or taken from No. 33-99, the southbound *Piedmont/Pan-American* and No. 34, the northward Piedmont. Also, for some years the L&N operated a pair of commuter trains, Nos. 9-12, between New Orleans and Ocean Springs, and more is written about that unusual service in the following pages.

Ron Flanary Photo

On August 12, 1966, veteran "Short Line" engineer C. Hagan "Jazzbo" Thompson prepared to climb into the cab of FP7 653 to take train 98, the northbound *Pan-American,* from Louisville to Cincinnati. The three coaches behind the FP7/E6 duo were deadheading to Cincy to bring Army inductees south the next day.

L&N Collection, UofL Archives

The *Eastern Express,* as Birmingham-Cincinnati train No. 8 was long called, steamed through suburban Anchorage, Ky., 12 miles northeast of Louisville on the Short Line to Cincy. The agent and a friend had stepped outside the gabled 1880s-vintage depot to watch No. 8's RPO snatch a pouch of mail. Traditional depot colors then (1940s): light olive with white trim.

L&N Collection, U of L Archives

Almost new *Humming Bird* streamliner halted momentarily on the Biloxi Bay MS. bridge in early 1947 for passenger department publicity art. Behind E7 780, consist included four full coaches, a coach-lounge, dining and tavern-lounge cars. Blue-silver scheme was replaced in early 1950s with solid blue.

L&N Collection, U of L Archives

So-called "head end" traffic—baggage, express, storage and sorted mail—for years contributed upwards of 35-40 per cent of L&N's total passenger revenues. Full Baggage 1404, a 70-foot long car, was being loaded at Union Station Louisville in 1935 for an outbound train.

St. Louis- Evansville -Nashville Line

Nos. 11-12 - Every third day streamlined *Dixie Flagler*, reserved seat coach and Pullman train between Chicago-Florida, using L&N from Evansville to Nashville. Offered fastest one-night out Midwest-Florida travel on "Dixie Route."

Nos. 51-52 - St. Louis-Evansville-Nashville through daytime local trains. Coaches only, connections in Evansville with LH&StL line trains to- from Louisville.

Nos. 53-92 - Remnants of old *Dixie Limited* on mostly nighttime schedules, St. Louis-Nashville, southward handling Chicago- and St. Louis-Nashville overnight sleepers.

Nos. 55-56 - St. Louis-Evansville night trains, handling Louisville-St. Louis overnight sleeper west of Evansville (LH&StL Line Nos. 155-156 worked car between Evansville-Louisville).

Nos. 80-81 - *Georgian*, Chicago-Evansville-Nashville—Chattanooga-Atlanta overnight train, with reserved seat coaches, diner and tavern-lounge, also Pullmans from Chicago and St. Louis to Atlanta; streamlined and diesel powered Jointly operated with C&EI, NC&StL, replacing old *Dixie Limited* on faster schedules.

Nos. 93-54 - *Humming Bird/Georgian* (Chicago-St. Louis section) connecting at Nashville with Nos. 5-6, mainline *Bird*, and handling through Chicago- and St. Louis-to-Gulf Coast Pullmans and reserved seat coaches between Nashville-St. Louis. Evansville-Chicago diner served breakfast, dinner on northward, southward trips, and St. Louis line through Sleeper and coach handled on same section, which also worked through cars off *Georgian*.

Nos. 94-95 - *Dixie Flyer*, once famous all-year Midwest-Florida train on slower two-nights out schedule, still offering through Pullman and coach service, with Evansville-Atlanta diner.

Cincinnati-Knoxville- Atlanta Mainline

Nos. 1-4 - Knoxville-Atlanta day locals, via Etowah-Blue Ridge and Marietta and scenic "Hook and Eye" Old Line (runs cut back to Copper Hill from Knoxville, discontinued altogether by 1951).

Nos. 17-18 - *Flamingo*, Cincinnati-Atlanta overnight trains, with Cincinnati-Knoxville and Cincinnati- and Louisville-Atlanta Pullmans (Louisville cars forwarded on Lebanon Branch trains Nos. 21-24 north of Corbin, Ky.), also coaches. An Atlanta- Etowah, Tenn., Dining car offered meals on the south end of the runs. Connections also at Corbin with early morning, late night Cumberland Valley branch trains (displaced by highway bus and discontinued altogether in 1958).

Nos. 29-30 - Cincinnati-Knoxville day local trains, connecting at Corbin with Lebanon Branch trains Nos. 22-23, to-from Louisville. Connection also at Winchester with Eastern Kentucky Division Branch trains Nos. 3-4, operating between Lexington-Hazard and Fleming, Ky. Nos. 29-30 came off in 1953.

Nos. 32-33 - *Southland*, long popular Chicago-Florida two nights out trains, by early 1950s serving West Coast of Florida with through Chicago- and Detroit- to St. Petersburg-Tampa and Sarasota through Pullmans, also through Cincinnati-West Coast-Florida coaches. PRR worked Chicago cars north of Cincy, with B&O moving Detroit car. Central of Georgia, ACL moved *Southland* below Atlanta, with FEC providing East Coast connection out of Jacksonville. Dining cars on Cincy-Macon day segment. In winter seasons prior to World War II, trains ran in two sections, serving both East, West Florida coasts.

New Orleans- Pensacola-Jacksonville

Nos. 60-61 - *Gulf Wind*, streamlined overnight Gulf Coast-West Florida trains, operated jointly with Seaboard Air Line RR between Chattahoochee-Jacksonville, Fla. All-room Jacksonville-New Orleans Pullmans, through reclining seat coaches (*Wind* cars moved on L&N's Nos. 99-34 between Flomaton, Ala.-New Orleans, with dining service offered by those trains. SAL diner between Jacksonville—Tallahassee).

Nos. 62-63 - Flomaton-Pensacola-Chattahoochee-Jacksonville day coach trains (also with SAL, east of Chattahoochee), connected with L&N Montgomery New Orleans main line trains at Flomaton, Al.

Nos. 64-65 - Selma- Flomaton, Al.- Pensacola day locals, also connecting at Flomaton with mainline Montgomery- New Orleans trains, including *Azalean, Humming Bird.*

Louisville-Frankfort- Lexington line

Trains 15-20, day locals between above cities.

Bowling Green-Memphis (Memphis Line)

Nos. 101-104 - Connected at Bowling Green, Ky., with Nos. 1—4, *Azalean*, to move overnight Cincinnati-Memphis sleepers.

Nos. 102-103 - Bowling Green-Memphis day locals, connecting at Bowling Green early morning, late evening with Mainline Mail-local trains Nos. 2-3.

Nos. 198-199 - Memphis section of *Pan-American*, handling through New York-Memphis Pullmans and through Cincinnati-Memphis coaches off mainline Pan south of Bowling Green, Ky.

H.L. Stuart Photo/Ron Flanary Collection
Below: After Cumberland Valley local passenger runs 11 and 12 had their western connection at Pineville amputated, this pitiful reminent continued as a Cumberland Gap, Tenn., to Norton, Va., run. In October 1952, train 12, at the joint N&W/L&N depot in Norton, was ready to roll. The Alco switcher/wood combine consist was more than adequate for the few passengers and "head-end" business. The trains came off for good in January 1953.

L&N and NC&StL operated these mixed trains in these states and on the following lines:

Alabama (L&N): Nos. 40-41, Bay Minette-Foley; Nos. 66-67, Selma-Myrtlewood; Nos. 160-161, Camden Branch (off Selma-Flomaton line); (NC&StL) Nos. 148-149, Decherd, Tn.-Huntsville, Ala.;

Georgia (L&N) Nos. 109-110, Blue Ridge, Ga.-Murphy, N.C.;

Illinois (L&N): Nos. 34-35, McLeansboro-Shawneetown;

Kentucky (L&N): Nos. 35-36, Louisville-Bardstown-Springfield; Nos. 164-169, Louis-ville-Shelbyville-Bloomfield;Nos. 203-4-5-6, Park City-Glasgow; Nos. 31-32, 40-41, Hart-ford-Earlington and Clay (MH&E Branch); Nos. 23-24, Elkton-Guthrie.

Tennessee (L&N): Nos. 303-304, Athens-Tellico Plains; Nos. 41-2-3-4, Gallatin-Hartsville-Scottsville, Ky.; (NC&StL): Nos. 161-162, Dickson-Hohenwahl (Centreville Branch); Nos. 146-147, Decherd -Lewisburg Branch (via Elora, Fayetteville); Nos. 188-189, Bridgeport, Ala.-Pikeville; Nos. 220-1, 224-5, Shelbyville Branch; Nos. 184-185, Tullahoma-Sparta (Sparta Branch); Nos. 132-133, Cowan-Tracy City-Palmer (Tracy City Branch).

L&N dining cars were famous for great food, and a happy passenger sampled one of the road's premiere meals, the "Country Ham Breakfast," which in addition to exclusive Duncan Hines hams featured "red eye" gravy and eggs. The scene also illustrated "Green Leaf" china used by the dining car department. Not marked "L&N," the pattern was a stock item produced by the Syracuse China Company. However, other table items such as silver flatware, coffee creamers, sugar bowls and water mugs were etched with the L&N logo.

Veteran mainline Conductor Henry Edmondson poses beside a "Pine" sleeper at Union Station, Louisville, in 1966. Even though patronage had fallen off drastically, L&N strove to provide a first-class passenger service.

Alabama Mineral Branch

Nos. 46-85, 47-86 - Birmingham-Gadsden-Anniston-Calera day local trains running on "loop" formed by AM Branch southeast of Birmingham.

Alabama & Florida Branch

Nos. 27-28, locals between Georgiana, Ala., and Graceville, Fla.

Nashville- Atlanta (NC&StL Main Line)

Nos. 3-4 - Overnight Nashville-Chattanooga-Atlanta mail trains, with Nashville-Atlanta sleeper and coaches, also making many intermediate stops.

Nos. 11-12 - *Dixie Flagler*, every third day Chicago-Miami coach-Pullman streamliner (see St. Louis-Nashville line).

Nos. 80- 80 - *Georgian*, overnight Chicago-Atlanta train.

Nos. 92-93 - *Dixie Limited*, through Chicago-Atlanta train, downgraded to mail-headend train after advent of *Georgian* on overnight schedules.

Nos. 94-95 - *Dixie Flyer*, once NC&StL's flagship train, also downgraded by *Dixie Flagler* and *Georgian* but still handling overnight Chicago-Atlanta cars and providing comfortable Nashville-Atlanta day service.

Nashville-Memphis (NC&StL Main Line)

Nos. 5-105, 6-106 - *City of Memphis* - Streamlined steam powered all-coach dayliner between Nashville-Memphis, via Bruceton, Lexington and Jackson, Tenn. Dining-lounge services also offered.

Nos. 1-101, 2-102 - Overnight Nashville-Memphis train, with Nashville-Memphis sleeper (l2 sec., drawing room), through coaches.

Hickman, Paducah Branch

Nos. 5-6, Bruceton, Tenn.- Hickman, Ky., day locals

Nos. 105-106, Bruceton, Tennn.- Paducah, Ky., day locals (Both sets of trains connected with *City of Memphis* streamliners at Bruceton, mornings and late afternoons.

In 1964, heavyweight coach #1909 was converted into a "rolling classroom" to introduce employees at all major terminals and yards to the then-new IBM "1050" computer system. The car from ACF in 1930 was renumbered, appropriately, 1050.

Bob Bell, Jr.

Standard heavyweight NC&StL coach 710, built by ACF in 1920 and modernized by the road's shops in 1937, was spotted at Nashville's Union Station in March 1957. After the 1940s, NC painted its passenger equipment dark blue with gold script lettering to match that of parent L&N.

L&N Collection, UofL Archives

"Jim Crow" combine no. 665, on the transfer table at South Louisville in 1953, gained fame as the "train" behind the restored "General" during the 1960s. As with other mixed train cars used in the South, the 665's center baggage section was divided by separate passenger sections for afro-americans and whites.

J. Parker Lamb

No. 95, the southbound *Dixie Flyer* curved through Wartrace, Tenn., in August 1963. Until the 1957 NC&StL merger, lead FP7 607 was a stranger on the Nashville-Atlanta main; its B-unit mate, the 1917, was of NC ancestry. Mostly a head-end train by then, Nos. 94-95 would be discontinued in January 1966.

The Long Decline

5

Consolidations, Reductions and Train-offs

In the immediate post-World War II years, most L&N branch and secondary lines offered some type of passenger service, either by a local passenger run or a mixed train (see sidebar for 1950 services). But, as automobiles and gasoline again became more plentiful, it was these train services, by then poorly patronized, which first fell victim.

Most of the mixed trains were discontinued by 1959, although well after the L&N-NC&StL merger, a half-dozen former NC mixed trains in Tennessee continued to run, protected by a Tennessee Public Service Commission order. So few were the patrons that the railroad accommodated them in cabooses outfitted with roll-over plush seats. L&N continued to offer the service into the 1960s, but, one by one, the trains went "freight only," the Commission relenting and relieving the L&N from the responsibility of maintaining such lightly used services (See Sidebar, L&N and NC&StL mixed trains, page 97).

Some mainline services were also reduced during the period, as certain trains were consolidated with sister runs to reduce costs yet still provide essential passenger services over principal routes. Between Montgomery-New Orleans, the southward *Pan-American* and *Piedmont Limited* ran as one train, after 1958. Northward, the *Pan* and *Crescent* combined, as did the southbound *Crescent* and *Humming Bird* after 1966, again, south of Montgomery.

Indeed, by the late-1950s and early 1960s, air, auto and bus competition combined had cut significantly into rail passenger traffic all over the US. Growing subsidies from all levels of government went toward new and improved airports and highway systems. The railroads' share of intercity and intrastate passenger travel, as high as 73 percent of all modes of transport during World War II, fell below 30 percent after 1960. In 1946 L&N passenger-miles-traveled totaled 1.3 billion. But by 1966, they had declined 85 percent, to 203 million miles!

For railroads like the L&N, the post-war era represented something of a paradox. On one hand, the new streamliners stimulated a positive, upbeat atmosphere; but on the other hand, traffic men and women viewed with dismay downward patronage levels on all trains, despite best efforts to continue their services. This sad paradox was illustrated by trains Nos. 15-20, running between Louisville and Lexington, via Lagrange and Eminence, Ky. Their predecessors, trains of the former Louisville & Frankfort RR, had run since 1851. Way back then, the running time between Louisville and Lexington (including change of trains in Frankfort) was 5 hours, 30 minutes, and the one way fare was $3.00. A century later (or in 1955, when Nos. 15-20 made their final runs), running times were 3 hours, 30 minutes and passengers paid $2.33 for a one way ticket. Obviously, rail fares simply had not kept pace with inflation, which was yet another aspect of the "passenger problem" faced by railroads.

Excursions, Reduced Fares and Snack Bars

Nonetheless, the L&N did not give up entirely. Economies and—where possible, improvements—were made to cut costs yet attract patronage. In 1959, two stainless steel diner-lounge cars were acquired from the

L&N Collection, U of L Archives

The first Saturday in May always brought a host of extra passenger trains and cars to Louisville for the Kentucky Derby. In May 1949 passengers off a special from Dallas-Ft. Worth basked momentarily in sunshine at Union Station before heading to Churchill Downs. *Derby Special* even had its own drumhead!

C&EI. Originally built for the Maine Central, the two cars went into service between Cincinnati-Montgomery on the *Pan-American*, offering a more realistic response to food and lounge services of the *Pan's* reduced passenger loads. In 1965, the two cars were further modified, becoming counter-lounge cars to make on-train food service even more cost-efficient. Also in early 1970, three coaches were outfitted with end-of-car snack bars to dispense an abbreviated sandwich-doughnut-refreshment service on the surviving St. Louis-Atlanta trains, Nos. 5-10.

Beginning in 1960, the L&N tried out a budget sleeping car plan. For example, coach fares plus space charges were offered on the Cincinnati-Memphis overnight sleeping car run. Moderately successful, the family plan and reduced individual round trip fares were extended to several other runs elsewhere in the system. Free coffee was also served to passengers on many trains throughout their runs.

Wanting to achieve maximum utilization of its passenger equipment, the L&N also strove to attract special travel to and from special events on- and off-line, such as the annual Kentucky Derby in Louisville and the New Year's Day Sugar Bowl game in New Orleans. Numerous excursions were operated during the years for railfan groups and other organizations, such as the well remembered "Round the Mountain" trips that ran many springs and falls from Atlanta into North Georgia and back. Also popular were the "Kiddie Specials," seasonal daytime runs out of Louisville that gave hundreds of school-aged children their first train ride and glimpse into the world of railroading.

By the early 1960s, the L&N also needed to purchase new equipment, what with extensive mileages accumulated by cars acquired just after World War II. The decision was made to upgrade rather than buy. During 1963 and 1964, the company rebuilt 64 cars in its South Louisville shops. The work included new seating and other internal improvements, disc brakes, electro-mechanical air conditioning equipment and repainting. Once overhauled, the cars went back into service on all trains operated on the L&N, C&EI and former NC&StL.

In addition to upgrading rolling stock (which included RPOs and other headend

Charles B. Castner/L&N Collection, UofL Archives
Amtrak's northbound *Floridian* stopped at the "new" Louisville station in late October 1976. The long consist included AutoTrain equipment coupled to the rear.

cars), the L&N also revamped its mail-handling facilities at several cities, in particular at Nashville, where a heavy volume of mail originated from the educational and publishing arms of the Southern Baptist denomination. At Nashville, $500,000 was invested in an automated mail system, which could handle 2400 mail bags per hour on a conveyor belt running directly from Union Station to the post office across the street.

Gulf Coast Commuters

L&N was never considered as a "commuter" railroad, even though in the 1920s and much earlier, the road (as did many other railroads) did in fact run short distance locals to and from the bigger on-line cities. The one surviving post-1920s commuter operation was a pair of Gulf Coast trains, Nos. 9 and 12, which ran between Ocean Springs, Ms., and New Orleans, a distance of 89 miles. Thanks to the inaccessibility of some Gulf communities, the locals survived as long as they did, providing a rush hour morning service to New Orleans, with an evening return to Ocean Springs. Fall 1953 schedules showed the trains taking two hours and twenty minutes for the

A cold rain added to the day's gloom as SDP40F 605 prepared to head the southward *Floridian* from Louisville's Union Station for the last time on October 31, 1976. Union's fine old train shed had already been dismanted. The next day, the train began calling at the Auto-Train terminal opposite Osborn Yard, on the city's south side.

89-mile run, making some 15-16 intermediate stops to pick up or drop passengers. Later, Nos. 9-12 were cut back to a Pass Christian, Ms.-New Orleans run of 63 miles, weekdays only. They made their last runs in 1965.

Oddly enough, commutation tickets were honored by L&N conductors on all trains in the so-called "commuter territory." Some Gulf Coast suburbanites were even known to ride to and from New Orleans on intercity trains; several like the combined *Piedmont/Gulf Wind* stopped regularly at Bay St. Louis,

Waveland and elsewhere to pick up or drop passengers to or from the Crescent City. And too, all L&N trains stopped at Carrollton Avenue, just a few minutes (and miles) out of the New Orleans Union Passenger Terminal. An unconditional stop for trains in both directions, Carrollton Avenue may well have been a "close in" suburban point.

During the 1960s, the *Pan, Georgian, Humming Bird, South Wind* and other trains soldiered on, still carrying respectable passenger loads. Most also handled much head-end

Full length NC&StL Railway Post Office 510, which ran for years on the *Dixie Flyer*, became L&N 1099 after the merger. The RPO was photographed in Louisville in 1968, the last year L&N was to run RPO cars.

Ed Bowers Photo

Southbound *Floridian* at Amqui, Tenn., near Nashville, on January 16, 1972, behind L&N GP30/ex-NYC E8 team.

traffic (mail and express) to help reduce operating losses. In 1961, L&N timetables advertised these trains: *Crescent, Georgian, Humming Bird, Gulf Wind, Pan—American, Piedmont, South Wind, Dixie Flyer and Flamingo.* But then, as the decade wore on, the once great trains came off, one by one. By 1968, the *Dixie Flyer, Flamingo* and *Piedmont Limited* had been discontinued, and that year,

C&EI cut its connection to the *Georgian.* L&N's remaining RPO cars made their last runs during 1968, as the Post Office Department shifted movement of first-class mail to air and highway. The loss of critical connecting traffic from its Chicago leg (C&EI) also badly hurt the *Humming Bird,* and that fine train made its last runs in early January 1969.

Jerry Mart/L&N Collection,
U of L Archives

Amtrak's *Floridian* became one of the most rerouted trains in that carrier's history. On August 2, 1974, the northbound train detoured by way of L&N's Evansville Division, from Nashville to Chicago. Bad track on Penn Central north of Louisville was given as the reason for the alternate routing. Two SDP40Fs led the train through Guthrie, KY.

The shortlived Louisville-Sanford, FL., *Auto-Train* suffered a number of setbacks, including several accidents. In winter 1974-75, three purple-red-and-white A-T U36B's crossed over Louisville Division main tracks to bring the run into its northern terminal.

More Reductions, One Addition

By spring 1969, only the *Gulf Wind, Pan-American* and *South Wind* remained in L&N timetables, along with a coach-only train between St. Louis and Atlanta. As expected, the public during those months leveled charges at the rail industry that train services were deliberately being downgraded. L&N President William Kendall, together with other rail CEOs, responded vigorously. With diminishing patronage, said Mr. Kendall, railroads were forced to take steps to reduce some services to offset revenue losses while continuing enough service to accommodate remaining passengers. The public, he added, often overlooked what railroads actually did to woo patronage long before they had to initiate service reductions. The shift of much mail and express traffic from trains to other modes in the 1960s also hurt the overall rail passenger picture. Further thrusts of subsidized air and highway competition brought the railroads' share of intercity travel to under 10 percent by the late 1960s.

Then, in November, 1969, Penn Central substituted a coach-only connection between Chicago-Louisville for the *South Wind*, forcing L&N to thereafter originate and terminate the Wind in Louisville. To cut losses but still provide a decent service, the L&N rescheduled the *Pan-American* to handle the *Wind's* cars between Louisville-Montgomery, and in the months following, L&N and SCL tried to continue a Midwest-Florida operation. But without the through Chicago-Florida cars, patronage dropped even more. The combined Pullman-coach operation (nicknamed by some the *South American*) continued until April 30, 1971.

Meanwhile, another service change actually produced an additional train for the L&N. With inclusion of C&EI's "eastern line" into the L&N system (trackage between Evansville-Woodland Junction, Ill.), Nos. 3-4 (former C&EI Danville-Chicago trains) appeared in the November 1969 L&N Timetable. Called the *Danville Flyer*, these 123-mile, long distance commuter runs offered daily coach and buffet-lounge service between Midstate Illinois communities and the Windy City. Nos. 3-4, last passenger trains on what was once a very busy C&EI main line, remained in L&N time tables until the advent of Amtrak.

So Long, Pan, Hello Amtrak

By the late 1960s, all passenger railroads of any size faced deficits which cut deeply into overall revenues. Those realities plus the domination of Interstate Highway travel led Congress to create in 1970 the National Railroad passenger Corporation. From that action, routes deemed essential and/or having potential for future ridership development were incorporated into the proposed Amtrak system; other remaining trains were discontinued, effective on Amtrak's startup date. Omitted from the new national network of services, the *Pan-American* and the St. Louis-Atlanta trains bowed out on April 30, 1971.

From May 1, 1971, on, the L&N participated with Amtrak in the operation of the *South Wind*, later renamed the Floridian, on the Chicago - Florida run. Much later, beginning in October 1980, L&N accommodated a Chicago-Indianapolis train between Crawfordsville-Maynard, In. From 1974 to 1977, the road also operated the Midwest section of Auto-Train between Louisville and Montgomery. These operations are more fully described in Chapter 5.

L&N passenger service by 1971 was but a pale reflection of what had been offered in 1940, or even 1961. But patrons then as now

Wm. C. Tayse/L&N Collection, UofL Archives

At its new southside Louisville terminal, the Midwest-Florida *Auto-Train* was positioned for loading on May 24, 1974, inauguration day for the new service. Just north of the station proper were ramps where cars of travelers were driven aboard auto-carriers.

On one of its last trips in early October 1979, the *Floridian*, northbound to Louisville, loaded passengers at Nashville's Union Station. The train was the last regularly scheduled run to call at the once busy terminal.

fondly remembered L&N for its clean, courteous and dependable service and the superb meals served in its dining cars. Recognition surely must go to countless men and women, living and deceased, who, over the years, gave life and purpose to this railroad's passenger service. Over telephones, at ticket and baggage counters, on trains, in dining cars and sleepers and in many other places little observed by the public, these employees served patrons ably and well and caused praise to be heaped on L&N passenger train travel.

Passenger Train Postscript

The *Floridian, Hoosier State* and *Auto-Train*

On Amtrak's startup date, May 1, 1971, the L&N was left with just one passenger operation, a restored daily Chicago-Florida *South Wind* which it operated between Louisville and Montgomery. The Chicago-Louisville segment was handled by the Penn Central, while the Montgomery-Jacksonville-Miami and West Coast legs were operated by Seaboard Coast Line. As it had done the previous 30 years, the L&N served as a bridge route for the Chicago - Florida train. The new consist was made up of three all-room sleepers (Chicago-Miami/Tampa cars), a full diner and reserved seat coaches. Added feature—a dome lounge-sleeper.

No one could have predicted in 1971 that this particular Amtrak route would experience so many changes during the coming decade. Initially, the *South Wind's* May 1971 schedule was the customary one-night-out between Chicago and Florida, a schedule which had existed since December 1940, when the three Florida streamliners (*Wind, Dixie Flagler* and *City of Miami*) went into service. But in November 1971, the "Wind" name was replaced by *Floridian* and a new schedule was introduced, offering two nights and one day between the Windy City and Sunny Florida. The train remained a PC-L&N-SCL operation over its traditional route. The two nights-one day schedule prevailed well into the next year, or until October 1972, when the train reverted back to the older one-night-out schedule.

That was not to last long, either. In April, 1973, the *Floridian* returned to its two nights and one day timing, only to swing again to the one-night-out schedule by December, then back to a two-night run by Spring 1974. The last-named schedule remained constant until October, 1976. Meanwhile, a route change was mandated by deteriorating track conditions on Penn Central, especially south of Indianapolis, where the *Floridian* had derailed some months before. In 1975 the train transferred to a new route between Louisville-Chicago, that of L&N's Monon Division, via Bloomington, Crawfordsville, Lafayette and Hammond, all in Indiana. There it remained until its last trips in October 1979.

Auto-Trains To Florida

Another passenger development occurred in May, 1974. That was when the Auto-Train Corporation began operation of a new Midwest—Florida train to complement its successful Northern Virginia-East Coast Florida service. L&N and SCL teamed up to move the train between a new terminal at Louisville and Sanford, Fla., Auto-Train's southern terminal. Equipment featured Auto-Train's white with red-and purple-trimmed sleepers, coaches and diners, with the boxcar-like auto carriers bringing up the rear. For its so-called "Midwestern terminal" at Louisville, Auto-Train built a new station, with covered platforms and the necessary loading ramps. The facility was located on the Louisville Division main line opposite L&N's Osborn Yard south of the city.

From 1974 to 1976, the Midwest *Auto-Train* ran in a variety of intervals and on schedules including tri-weekly, twice-weekly, and even once a week. However, the traffic potential of the run never fully developed to Auto-Train's satisfaction, and for several reasons. For one, the combined L&N-SCL route was longer, with profiles far more difficult to operate over (especially on L&N's side) than on the east coast raceway. Consequently, the roads had difficulty in maintaining decent running times and in arriving "on—time" for the critical one-night-out schedule. Inaccessibility of the Louisville Terminal, situated as it was some distance from the city and well off the Interstate corridor, may also have figured adversely in the train's success as did erratic intervals for the train's trips.

Amtrak Plus Auto-Train Equals…

This brings us to 1976, when *Auto-Train* and Amtrak signed an agreement to combine the *Auto-Train* service and the *Floridian* between Louisville and Sanford on L&N and SCL. In order to coordinate the combined Amtrak-Auto-Train operation, the *Floridian* returned to a one-night-out schedule. At Louisville, Amtrak left stately old Union Station downtown for the last time on October 31

(1976) to run the *Floridian* in and out of the new Auto-Train facility on the city's south side. There, the Auto-Train cars were picked up for the run south to Florida, and conversely, dropped on the northward leg. Amtrak continued to use the Louisville facility until the *Floridian* was discontinued in October 1979.

The combined *Auto-Train/Floridian* made an impressive sight indeed as it highballed in and out of Louisville. Both Amtrak and Auto-Train supplied motive power; Amtrak E8s tied on to the distinctive Auto-Train U-Boat units to wheel the long train, which often ran to more than 30 cars. Equipment included the auto carriers and baggage cars, coaches, diners, lounge cars, and sleepers. Amtrak and Auto-Train sections were separated, passengers from one section not allowed access to the other section.

The one-night schedule for the combined trains remained in effect through 1977, or until the Amtrak-Auto-Train agreement was cancelled. As with Auto-Train's earlier experience, the two carriers, with the operating railroads, found it difficult to maintain schedules as well as make the regular intermediate stops for Amtrak passengers. Acceleration from those stops also took longer, because of the great weight and length of the combined train. Again, traffic potential on the Auto-Train side did not materialize, and after 1977, the *Floridian* returned to its slower two-nights out schedule.

Floridian Finis, Hoosier State Start-up.

Then in 1979, the *Floridian* became entangled in the Department of Transportation's controversial train-off campaign, which was motivated by Carter Administration budget cuts. Together with several other long-distance Amtrak trains, the *Floridian* was positioned on the lower side of Amtrak's list of train loadings. The scheduling flip-flops, route changes, poor time keeping and the Auto-Train experiment had taken their toll in riders since 1971. And, while new SDP40 units had replaced the aging E-units as motive power, the venerable Heritage cars assigned to the train left much to be desired, in mechanical reliability and passenger comfort.

An abbreviated Hoosier State waited for the "All Aboard" from Union Station, Indianapolis, in July 1983.

Last ditch campaigns in various on-line cities and states were staged to save the service, but the *Floridian* did not survive, making its last trips on October 9, 1979. Its demise marked the first time in the long history of the L&N that a regularly scheduled passenger train was not in service somewhere on the system. The L&N continued to be listed in the Amtrak System time table, even without a train. The October 28, 1979 issue listed trains 317 and 318 between Chicago and Indianapolis with no schedule but with the following statement: "Service to commence on a date to be announced. Call Amtrak's toll-free number for information."

Train Nos. 317 and 318 became the *Hoosier State* and on October 1, 1980, began running daily over L&N and Conrail trackage. The L&N (now CSX Transportation) handled the trains between Crawfordsville and Maynard, Indiana. Between Crawfordsville and Indianapolis, they operated over tracks of the former Peoria & Eastern, a New York Central subsidiary (Conrail). North of Maynard, the trains used the former Logansport line of the Pennsy (also Conrail). To accommodate the new runs, L&N upgraded trackage north of Crawfordsville, installing new ties, laying welded rail and upping track speeds to 80 mph for much of the

way. Later in the 1980s, Amtrak also shifted its tri-weekly Chicago-Washington *Cardinal* from a Chessie route to the former Monon trackage between Crawfordsville-Maynard. The move gave Indianapolis-Chicago travelers a choice of several schedules.

With the advent in 1984 of the New Orleans Worlds Fair, L&N also hosted another Amtrak train, the *Gulf Breeze*, running between Mobile and New Orleans from April until the following winter. The train attempted to capture Fair-related travel between Gulf Coast communities and the Crescent City, and its funding was shared by the three participating states, Alabama, Louisiana and Mississippi. Regrettably, requests to continue funding for the trains beyond 1985 were not answered. However, by the late 1980s, Amtrak did restore passenger service to Mobile from another direction, Birmingham and Montgomery. A day-time service connecting with the *Crescent* at Birmingham went on, to bring back passenger travel to that important Alabama intercity corridor. Alas, budget woes at Amtrak in 1995 cut short that service and its potential for extension. The Indianapolis-Chicago *Hoosier State* suffered a like fate, being discontinued in September 1995.

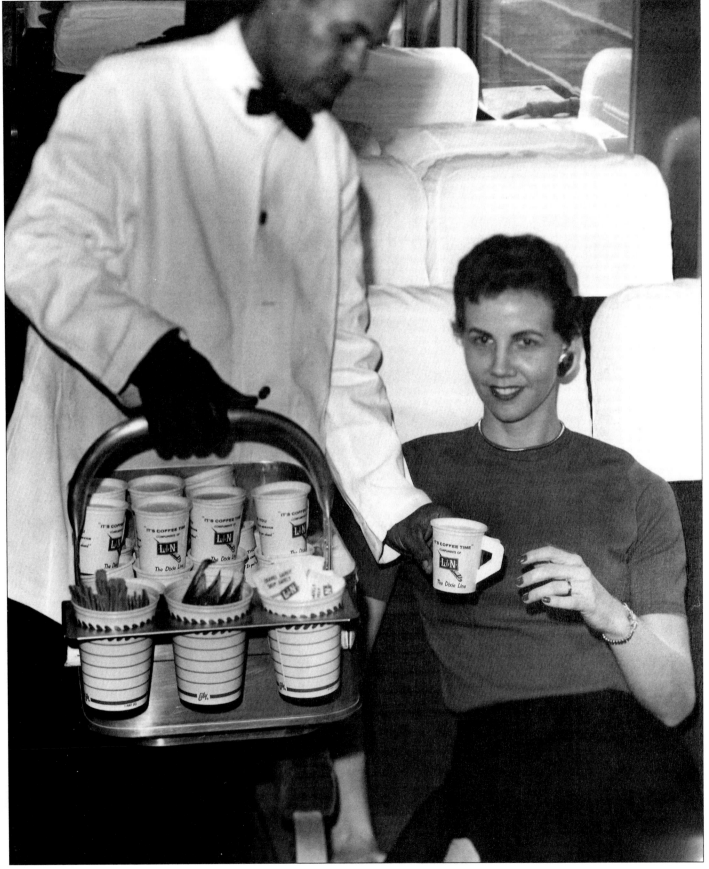

C. Norman Beasley/L&N Collection, UofL Archives

"It's Coffee Time on the Dixie Line." Long before airline stewardesses served up java to air travelers, the L&N provided complimentary coffee to its passengers.

In October 1954, J. B. Hagan, agent-operator at Lebanon Junction, Ky., forked up orders to a crew member in the cab of northbound local No. 32. Advent of CTC in the decade ahead eliminated such scenes as this.

Tonnage Between the Great Lakes and the Gulf Coast

6

The L&N: Super Freight Hauler might well have sufficed as an alternate title for this chapter. It is true that L&N over time did develop and operate a considerable systemwide passenger service. By and large, however, it was freight that sustained the road, decade after decade, generating well over three-fourths of all total revenues. After 1900, of course, coal became the top commodity transported, in terms of revenues generated and tonnages handled. L&N's long relationship with King Coal is more fully described in Chapter 8.

Historical Perspective

Even before the first wheels turned, L. L. Robinson, L&N's then-chief engineer, wrote prophetically (in 1854) about the freight traffic potential of his new railroad. From preliminary surveys and studies of what might move by rail, Robinson estimated that significant revenues could well come from farm crops, timber, livestock and manufactures, all from on-line counties and communities. The new railroad, he believed, could also profit from distributing to those same areas coal from northeastern mines; such coal heretofore had moved into Kentucky and Tennessee by river and then inland by wagons and carts over crude roads.

As to through traffic, Robinson cited the strategic position the L&N would soon occupy, and he listed some 24 rail and river connections at the two main termini as well as diverging branch lines, which were also anticipated to feed and/or receive a sizeable volume of traffic. Robinson singled out cotton from West Tennessee and Mississippi and grains from Illinois and Indiana as potentially moving in great quantity over L&N rails. He also foresaw

a challenge to the Ohio River for its traffic. "It may be inferred," Robinson wrote his management and directors, "that your road will command traffic between the four important converging points of Memphis, Nashville, Louisville and Cincinnati."

In actuality, L&N, almost from its inception as a regional carrier, was destined to serve far beyond Kentucky and Tennessee. The Civil War (1861-65) saw to that. Early on, L&N funneled men and materiel to the Confederate states, and the principal part of revenues it earned in 1860-61 came from freight transported south. After 1862, of course, the tonnage continued southward but in support of the advancing Union offensive into Tennessee, Georgia and Alabama.

Even before the conflict ended, President James Guthrie and fellow officers looked toward expanding the L&N's territory and increasing its freight traffic base. Wartime revenues permitted (in 1864) construction to begin, to extend the Lebanon branch toward the Southeastern Kentucky coal fields and beyond to Knoxville and rail connections there.

Just after war's end, Guthrie and his management also anticipated the great potential the "Memphis Line" possessed, once the two connecting roads, Memphis & Ohio and Memphis, Clarksville & Louisville, were fully repaired and again operating. Even as loans flowed from Louisville to the M&O and MC&L to insure their reconstruction, advantages of the new route were being publicized

Operations between the three "Memphis Line" participants, meanwhile, were being coordinated so that, as L&N's 1866 Annual Report announced, "It is hoped that this arrangement, when fully known among businessmen, will induce a large amount of freight

A New Orleans-bound freight powered by a 700-series 2-8-0 hustled along flat Southern Mississippi farmland in early view from about 1912.

to go over our line." Negotiations also led to an interchange at Humboldt, Tenn., with the Mobile & Ohio and Mississippi Central for freight destined to the Gulf Coast.

While the L&N continued to develop local traffic, it was to the long distance hauls and expansion into new territories that its management looked for new traffic. President Guthrie was prompted to write in the company's 1868 annual report thusly: "Formerly a local road doing business between Louisville and Nashville, we are now competing with the various other transportation companies for the through traffic of the entire South." A year later, his successor, Horatio Newcomb could declare to L&N directors that "the increase in the revenue from southbound freight, both from Louisville to Nashville and via the Memphis Branch to the Southwest is due to the increased prosperity of the country and also to the improved facilities which are now offered for the trans-shipment of freight by this company and its connecting lines." By "improved facilities," President Newcomb was referring to several so-called "fast freight lines"

(noted in more detail below) which had just been formed to expedite traffic to and from southern cities.

Author and transportation historian Maury Klein has observed that "the gradual shift in emphasis from local to through traffic constituted the most significant factor in southern railway strategy." For emerging systems such as the L&N, Klein believed that such a shift and its related growth took form in several ways-through cooperation, consolidation and construction. An example of cooperation, said Klein, was L&N's participation in the "Green Line," which, with neighboring lines, sought to expedite freight shipments and car movements between Louisville, Charleston, S.C., Macon, Ga., and other southern cities.

Improved service was achieved by means of coordinated freight train schedules between carriers and closer connecting times at interchange points. The similar "Louisville & Gulf Line" strove to speed up freight movements between Louisville, Mobile, New Orleans, Selma and Vicksburg. The later formation (in 1875) of the Southern Railway & Steamship

L&N and other railroads long maintained large city freight stations to receive, store and transload freight. Pictured was the New Orleans freight station about 1925.

Association was intended to extend cooperation by the participating carriers into the realm of rate-making (interested readers are referred to Dr. Klein's book, *Unfinished Business: The Railroad in American Life*; Press of New England, 1994, for a more detailed description of strategies followed by southern-region railroads).

Consolidation (of rail lines) and new construction became other strategies the L&N and related roads pursued during the 1870s and 1880s, states Klein. Such tactics were taken not only to enter new geographic territories but also to protect that expansion and command the new traffic, freight and passenger, that was produced. In the L&N's case, that translated into leasing the Nashville & Decatur and constructing unfinished segments of the South & North Alabama (between Calera and Decatur) to reach the vast coal and mineral

wealth of North and Central Alabama.

During the three decades, 1870-1900, the L&N also sought to expand its freight traffic base through purchasing adjacent lands and enticing new settlers and industries to those properties. During the 1870s and 80s in North Alabama, notably at Cullman, and in West Florida, the road helped settle large numbers of families of foreign origin in on-line communities, to which industries were soon after to locate. Those pre-1900s developments were conducted by the road's general immigration and industrial department, which in 1903 was reorganized and expanded in its mission and outreach. More intensive promotion followed, to acquaint prospects with the merits of L&N's territory and to the types of products suited to particular regions. From that pioneering work evolved the Industrial Development Department and its more recent activities

117

cooperating with on-line communities to identify suitable sites and lure new industries to them.

Anticipating great industrial growth for what was soon to become Birmingham and environs, L&N in the 1870s went so far as to acquire a great deal of nearby property containing vast deposits of coal, iron ore and limestone. All three ingredients, conveniently found in great quantities and easily retrieved by rail, were crucial for steel making. It was natural that steel mills and mining operations would follow. As a consequence, the L&N sold most of the above properties to then-developing steel and coal interests and focused on providing adequate transportation.

One of the great boosters of that development was L&N's own president, Milton H. Smith (1884-6, 1891-1921). First serving as local freight agent in Louisville just after the Civil War, Smith advanced to the position of General Freight Agent by 1869, remaining in that important office until 1878. During that period, he introduced many of the policies which boosted the growth and prosperity of Birmingham and its developing industries.

Smith introduced a sliding scale of rates and tariffs for steel and iron traffic. When the pig iron market was depressed and iron prices dropped, he directed that rates be lowered to enable Birmingham-area iron and steel to better compete with comparable products in other markets. When business and demand improved, freight rates were increased accordingly. Smith was remembered especially for his encouragement to area coal and iron men during those depressed times. "Keep in blast," he told them. "It doesn't make a bit of difference what the freight rate is; keep in blast! I'll carry the product to market on my back if I have to!"

Commodity Pies and Traffic Trends

Fortunately, the diversity of the 13-state region served by the L&N long provided it with a broad mix of freight traffic sources,

from a variety of manufactured goods produced by industries, to the agricultural produce of farms and the wood products from forest and timberlands, the last named which also proliferated across much of L&N's territory. Several samplings from different years serve to illustrate L&N's so-called "Commodity Pie." In 1921, L&N tonnage fell into four main classifications:

1- Products of mines, chiefly bituminous coal, iron ore and coke;
2- Agricultural products, including corn, cotton, fruits, tobacco and vegetables;
3 - Manufactures; and
4 - Lumber and forest products.

In 1921, Coal and coke together represented about two-thirds of the total tonnages, also contributing about half of all freight revenues. Annual tonnages during the early 1920s totaled some 43 million tons.

By 1967, the L&N "commodity pie" and its percentages of total revenues had changed significantly: Manufactures -including grain mill products, paper, chemicals, electrical machinery, primary and fabricated metal products- contributed approximately 58 per cent; Mineral products, including bituminous coal, 32 per cent; forest products and lumber, 5 per cent; and farm products, 5 percent. The L&N operated an extensive freight train service to move these commodities, and the various divisional train services were coordinated, one with another, throughout the system. Interestingly enough, after 1900 and its growth to full maturity, L&N was considered a traffic-originating road, generating from its own lines a significant percentage of the total tonnages handled- some years as high as 90 per cent.

While the directional flow of much L&N freight traffic was to the south during the formative decades (1850s to 1880s), new traffic patterns after 1900 transformed the L&N into a "northbound" railroad, that is, one on which freight traffic moved predominately from south to north. With development of the Birmingham coal and steel districts and the Eastern and

&N's first named fast freight, the *Silver Bullet*, climbed Sand Mountain in Northern Alabama about 1940. Auxillary water tender behind the -4 Mikado helped train make fast schedule.

Western Kentucky coal fields, immense tonnages of coal and raw steel, for example, rolled north to Midwestern industries and power plants. The demand for agricultural and food products as well as for paper and timber also remained strong in Midwestern and Northeastern markets. And too, considerable import traffic rolled northward from Gulf Coast ports over L&N routes.

Two important freight service improvements were made by the L&N during the Depression-1930s to offset traffic losses and inroads of highway truck competition. In March 1933, the road inaugurated free pick-up and delivery service for less-than-carload (LCL) shipments moving within a radius of 230 miles. Reception from shippers for the service (which was offered from nearly 500 stations) was generally favorable, and, beginning in January 1936, free pickup for most all LCL shipments was introduced by the railroad, regardless of distances involved.

Then in fall 1936, the L&N launched a fast freight service from Cincinnati and Louisville to the Gulf port cities of Mobile, New Orleans and Pensacola to forward high value merchandise between those points. Named the *Silver Bullet*, the new train (No. 71 to operating folk) offered late afternoon departures from Ohio Valley cities and second morning delivery at the Gulf Ports. It became one of the faster long distance freight trains then operating in the United States. As such, No. 71 (the *Bullet*) was required to reel off a demanding 35-hour schedule for its 925-mile trip, and to further expedite running times, L&N "mainlined" No. 71 through major terminals, stopping there only to swap crews and engines. The road also equipped the assigned motive power - J-4 class heavy Mikados and H-29A Consolidations (the latter used south of Mobile)—with auxiliary tenders to eliminate intermediate water stops. Employment of night warehouse forces, faster preparation of waybills and alert dispatching also helped the train maintain its speedy service.

J-4 Mikado 1862 rolled a Louisville Division main stem freight southward toward Bowling Green, Ky., in January 1951. Big J-4 Mikes were L&N's standard system heavy freight hauler for almost 30 years.

The woodracks arrived in Pensacola's Goulding Yard in 1950 behind J-3 class Mike 1548. Logs on racks were destined for area paper mills.

Wm. C. Tayse
L&N Collectio/University of Louisville Archives

Retarder operator at Radnor Yard, Nashville, slowed cut of hoppers moving through group retarderon way into classification yard: April 1958. Expanded and modernized during 1952-4, Radnor became L&N's first semi-automated freight yard.

J. Parkert Lamb

"Extra 417 North" destined for Birmingham picked up speed after leaving Montgomery's S&N Yard in June 1954. Three clean GP7s headed the run.

New steam power, in shape of 42 M-1s delivered during and just after World War II, helped speed up Cincy, CV and EK schedules. M-1 1954 started Atlanta-bound fast freight No. 45 from DeCoursey Yard, Ky., in early 1950s.

Girding for the War

L&N's freight traffic patterns were to change again—and dramatically so—with the onset of World War II (1941-45) and the post-war decades which followed. In the several years of mobilization just before the war, new and reactivated military camps and new defense industries across the South began to generate sizeable tonnages. For the L&N, increased traffic on many of its divisions, sub-divisions and branches materially reduced empty car movements (traditionally, cars moving on the southward or return leg), as the volume of new loads—many with defense ship-

ments moving south—grew to equalize cars moving northward.

One element of terminal planning, conceived in the months just before World War II, was to pay off handsomely during and after the conflict. That was the expansion and upgrading in 1941 of DeCoursey Yard, the important Cincinnati gateway facility situated just south of Covington, Ky. DeCoursey, built in the 'teens, sat at the hub of mainlines coming north from Atlanta and the Eastern Kentucky coal fields as well as from Louisville, Memphis and the Gulf Coast. Handling upwards of 40 trains a day in and out, the big yard ranked as one of L&N's most important terminals. All traffic northward to the Cincinnati gateway was classified at DeCoursey for delivery to local industries or interchange to other railroads.

The DeCoursey upgrading included the addition of more tracks as well as the installation of a hump and retarder operation for the north yard, first of its kind on the L&N. The improvements also speeded up freight train scheduling and the local deliveries of cars and greatly reduced interchange times with Cincinnati area railroads.

World War II impacted tremendously on the L&N's freight traffic. The company handled more traffic in 1942 than during any previous year. Over 71 million tons of freight rolled across L&N Land in '42, and had it not been for the improvements at DeCoursey yard, traffic flow through the Cincy gateway would have been seriously hampered. Even higher totals were recorded in 1943 and 1944, some 73 million tons for the latter year. Those peak traffic levels taught L&N men much about the capacity and the limits of their railroad. At war's end in 1945, they began making plans to improve services for a nation at peace.

Peace-time and More Silver Bullets

L&N positioned itself in the postwar decades to capitalize on the expanding national economy. The road's long range planning

With transfer run, Baldwin switcher and crew waited in clear for arriving northbound freight train behind a J-4 Mikado at South Louisville Yard, Louisville, about 1950.

Schedules of *Silver Bullet*, other fast freights, benefitted significantly, as L&N dieselized in 1950s. The *Bullet*, behind an F7 trio, rolled through downtown Birmingham on its way south.

was on-going, manifesting itself in new train services, improved yards and terminal facilities, communications and signals, equipment tailored for shipper needs, addition of new motive power and vigorous industrial development promotion throughout the South. The Sunbelt's great growth also continued well beyond the 1940s, thanks in part to abundant resources of raw materials, fresh water, manpower and moderate climate the southern states possessed.

In his magazine-length essay on the L&N in TRAINS (March 1955), Editor David P. Morgan describes the shift underway."Its (L&N's) territory, for years a pretty but essentially rural locale, is still as pretty as ever, but TVA, war and industrial decentralization have combined to place the emphasis on the factory instead of the farm … and you can spot what economists call 'growth areas' on the booming docks at Mobile and New Orleans, in the hamlets where silver factory stacks are going up behind L&N's little gray and white frame stations, and—above all—in once—sleepy cities."

In 1946, new freight services were announced and implemented. Schedules were created from Atlanta and its connections to Cincinnati, providing third morning delivery of Florida perishable traffic there and fourth morning delivery at Chicago, Detroit, Toledo, and Cleveland. A faster southbound schedule

was also established from Cincinnati to Atlanta and connections beyond, offering second morning delivery to Albany and Macon, Ga., and Jacksonville, Fl.

On the Main Stem, the *Silver Bullet*, inaugurated in 1936, continued its sprint from Cincinnati and Louisville to New Orleans. Overnight fast freights were also introduced between these cities: Montgomery and New Orleans, 318 miles; Cincinnati and Knoxville, 292 miles; Cincinnati and Nashville, 297 miles; East St. Louis and Louisville, 314 miles; and Nashville and Montgomery, 302 miles. The new trains not only helped to retain existing traffic, but also brought new business to the L&N during the late 1940s and early 1950s. However, other changes and improvements lay ahead.

New Yard For Nashville

Anticipating merger with the NC&StL, the L&N in 1952 began expanding and upgrading its Radnor Yard in Nashville. Goal of the project was to combine Nashville terminal operations of the two railroads. Since World War I, L&N had originated and terminated its freight trains at Radnor Yard, on the city's south side, while the NC&StL used an even older yard downtown at Union Station. Under that two-yard system, interchange of freight between

L&N and NC&StL required 18 hours on the average, a growing disadvantage by the 1950s, compared with timing truckers offered. Also by then, the existing yards had become inadequate to handle the longer diesel-powered trains both roads operated.

L&N opened its "new" Radnor Yard in September 1954; The expanded facility was made up of a 13-track receiving yard, a 56-track hump classification yard (with semi-automated retarders), and a 22-track departure yard. The yard also contained car repair tracks, new diesel shop and servicing tracks, platforms for icing refrigerator cars, livestock pens, as well as yard office and tower, retarder operator towers and a new freight house to replace aging structures downtown. Benefits to the shipping public were quick to come. Traffic moving between the two roads came to be promptly swapped at Radnor, greatly reducing interchange times.

Equipment repairs were likewise concentrated at one facility, as was servicing of motive power. Valuable downtown property formerly occupied by NC&StL's old yard was released for industrial development.

During the 1950s, L&N strove to improve its LCL freight business with new overnight services between Louisville and Birmingham. Forwarder traffic also was growing and by the mid-50s had increased some 250% over 1946 traffic levels. It was then too that L&N took its first small steps into the realm of intermodal traffic, namely, piggyback. During August 1955, several test shipments of single trailers on flatcars rolled south from Louisville to Birmingham and New Orleans. The great growth of L&N's piggyback and broader intermodal services is outlined in the next chapter.

An unusual traffic opportunity presented itself during the 1950s. Birmingham- area steel companies began purchasing iron ore from Venezuela, the ore arriving by ocean shipping at Mobile. Much ore came directly to U.S. Steel Company's push-button ore-handling conveyor-belt on the Alabama State Docks. With its Sibert yard next door, L&N got in on a sizeable share of the South American ore traffic, and in order to better handle the traffic, the road purchased 250 ore cars (each of 95-ton capacity) from Pullman Standard. The new cars, 36 feet long versus 24 feet for Lake

Alco FA-2 cab units sped north from Atlanta in April 1952 with perishibles from Florida destined for Midwestern markets.

Superior region cars, were based on Pullman's successful PS-3 hopper design but with a number of modifications.

Over the next decade, the L&N transported between 6 and 10 million tons of iron ore annually between the port of Mobile and Birmingham area; tonnages varied with fluctuations in steel production. Much later, Birmingham mills began receiving needed ore in all-rail shipments from Minnesota's Mesabi Range via a Duluth, Mesabi & Iron Range-Wisconsin Central and CSXT routing.

Many factors combined to help L&N improve freight services during the 1950s, but if one factor could be singled out, surely it was the shift from steam power to diesel. That was accomplished in late 1956, when the remaining steam locomotives still at work on the former Cincinnati Division were sidelined. Chapter 9 more fully traces L&N's motive power story, detailing the shift from steam to diesel. Suffice it here to note that diesels, offering far greater availability and utilization as well as the capacity to handle longer trains at faster speeds, fully commended themselves to a cost-conscious L&N management for all classes of service.

New Yards For the South and Midwest

More terminal improvements, meanwhile, followed in the wake of the Radnor Yard opening at Nashville. In 1957, L&N completed modernization of the former NC&StL Hills Park Yard on Atlanta's northwest side. The work included a 24-track classification yard and hump, with room for expansion; a seven-track departure yard; and 11 tracks in a receiving and "hold" yard. The enlarged sub—yards raised overall capacity of the facility to 2,000 cars per day. Mechanical facilities there were likewise improved.

L&N also transferred its Atlanta terminal operations from the smaller Hulsey Yard of the Georgia RR downtown to the more expansive Hills Park, which was renamed Tilford Yard to honor President John E. Tilford. The addition of eight more tracks in the "Bowl" or classification yard and a larger master retarder along with several other additions and track changes, all in 1964-5, increased Tilford's per-day capacity to 3,000 cars.

Right on the heels of the Atlanta improvements came a new hump yard at Birmingham. There, new classification, departure and

Jill Oroszi

South Louisville-built steel caboose brought up rear of Nashville-to-Atlanta fast freight No. 683, as it joined Atlanta Division tracks from the Radnor Yard connection: May 1981.

Loaded L&N hoppers and their contents helped fuel blast furnaces of Republic Steel Co.'s modern Gadsden, Ala., plant in this 1965 view. Hoppers in foreground moved slag, byproduct of steel-making process.

receiving yards were carved out of the Alabama hills just north of the original Boyles yard, roundhouse and car shop. Opened in 1959, the new Boyles Yard could classify up to 4,200 cars per day. Normal operation called for 3,500 cars to be channeled through the yard. Capacity of the "bowl" was 1,500 cars, handled through five groups of eight tracks each. At Boyles, the new hump yard featured such advances as automatic route systems using coded, pre-punched tape and closed circuit television to check inbound freight trains.

From Nashville to Atlanta to Birmingham, each of these new yards was more advanced than its previous sisters.

L&N's philosophy of freight service operations in the post World War II decades centered around modern yard facilities at strategic on-line cities, and next to be upgraded was the terminal at Chattanooga. There, in 1960-61, L&N vacated NC&StL's cramped Cravens Yard and its old downtown Freight House in favor of a new flat yard at Wauhatchie, in the broad valley just north of Lookout Mountain. Smaller than Boyles or Tilford, Wauhatchie Yard consisted of three long receiving and forwarding tracks and 14 classification tracks. The long receiving tracks made it possible for through freights to pick up or set off cars for area industries. A new yardmaster's tower, freight house, offices, car- and diesel shop rounded out the new features at Wauhatchie, which was designed for a maximum working capacity of 2,500 cars per day.

Another medium sized flat yard, Atkinson at Madisonville, Ky., was upgraded during 1963 to aid the Western Kentucky coal industry. As revised, Atkinson's South Yard contained 12 tracks, while its North Yard was given eight; total capacity of the 2.7-mile long facility was 1,334 cars. A high-capacity track-weigh scale, new yard office and diesel servic-

David Oroszi
Bound for Birmingham, fast freight No. 470 rumbled through turn span across the Pascagoula River at Pascagoula, Miss., in October 1981.

128

Cincinnati-bound *Dixie Jet,* behind brand new GP30s, swung through Anchorage, Ky., in August 1962.

ing facilities were also part of the improvements, all of which were intended to relieve congestion and improve coal movements through that important West Kentucky—Evansville Division hub.

The mammoth DeCoursey Yard near Cincinnati also came in for expansion between 1961-1964. A new southbound hump and "bowl" yard with 24 classification tracks were built, making DeCoursey L&N's largest freight terminal and the only one with twin humps and "bowls." New departure and receiving yard tracks next to the south "bowl" yard also speeded up train handling, while new "state of the art" computer and telecommunications systems greatly enhanced staff workflow, at the same time improving car utilization. An engine underpass with 26-foot clearance, unique to L&N yards, led directly under the south hump to connect departure and receiving yard tracks with the diesel terminal, which with its shop and servicing tracks replaced the old steam-era roundhouse. The new improvements increased DeCoursey's handling capacity to 7,200 cars per day.

At Sibert Yard in Mobile, a 1967 upgrading brought track changes, along with a new Yardmaster's Tower, crew facilities and a Customer Service Center, which concentrated under one roof all area employees whose work had some bearing on L&N's traffic moving to, through and from Mobile. Working as a team, Center staff accumulated, processed and offered accurate service data to all area shippers. The Customer Service Center concept evolved at Radnor Yard in Nashville the year before. Its success led to CSCs being eventually established not only at all of the L&N's city terminals but in Louisville in a system-overview role. The CSCs also represented a major change in rail freight customer relations, as L&N and sister roads lines shifted agents and other staff from rural or outlying depots to central locations equipped with the latest telecommunications technologies.

Skillman, a brand new flat yard albeit small in size, was created out of Ohio River Valley farmlands at Hawesville, Ky., in 1968 to serve the growing aluminum and paper industries nearby. And, in the wake of the 1969 C&EI merger, L&N revamped the former C&EI's Brewer Yard in Danville, Ill. At Brewer, nine new and longer tracks replaced 16 shorter, more cramped tracks, and agency and supervisory staff were moved from other locations into a new yard office.

A whopper of a shipment, huge isocracking reactor vessel for the Fluor Corp., Ltd., rolled south from Chattanooga in March 1963 aboard two heavy duty flat cars. At its local plant, Combustion Engineering, Inc., fabricated one million-ton shipment, which L&N-ACL moved, via a special Atlanta-Birmingham route, to the Gulf Coast.

Wm. C. Tayse/L&N Collection/University of Louisville Archives

Sibert, on Mobile's industrial east side, was L&N's principal Gulf Coast classification yard. Next door to Alabama State Docks, left, yard was upgraded in 1960s.

Also in the 1960s, L&N introduced an intermodal distribution service called BIDS for liquid and dry bulk products. New terminals were built in Atlanta, Louisville, and New Orleans, where covered hoppers and tank cars could be spotted for clean and efficient transfer of cargoes to or from highway trucks. Joint rates with highway carriers were established for movement to non-rail points up to 200 miles from the terminal. Promotion of the Bids service brought a variety of commodities back to rail.

Dixie Jets and Runthroughs

For many years, the L&N operated just one "named" freight train, the previously mentioned *Silver Bullet*. In mid-1962, the road launched a new "named" hotshot, the Birmingham-New York City runthrough *Dixie Jet*, which operated via Cincinnati and a PRR connection to provide third morning delivery in Manhattan (and in Birmingham, on the southbound move). The *Jet* was a forerunner of more runthrough freight trains L&N was to introduce in the decades ahead via other gateways and connecting railroads, notably at

Atlanta (with SCL), Memphis (Cotton Belt and MoPac), New Orleans (SP) and Woodlawn, Ill. (BN).

Moderate hilly to mountainous terrain encountered in Kentucky, Tennessee, North Alabama and Georgia held down L&N freight trains to moderate speeds. The operating department set track speeds, terrain permitting, at 50 mph for fast freights, and 60 mph for all-piggyback or other intermodal trains. L&N freight trains were scheduled in the division time tables as first, second, and third class trains with designations as piggyback, fast freight, and local freights. This permitted tighter quality control in so far as train schedules were concerned. A divisional numbering system was also introduced, to improve train identification.

System Service Center

On the L&N as elsewhere in railroading, freight train operations were and continue to be the so-called "production line," providing needed transportation services to customers. However, necessary behind-the-scenes activity was also required to translate train movements

C. Norman Beasley/L&N Collection/University of Louisville Archives

Carmen swapped truck on tank car in new enclosed running repair shop at Louisville's Osborn Yard.

Louisville's four-mile long Osborn Yard ireplaced smaller Strawberry, Yard, satellite facilities in 1977-9. Classification or "bowl" yard, center, contained 57 tracks; departure yard tracks, Auto-Amtrak station were at left.

into dependable, efficient service. That service also depended on close cooperation between key departments, especially marketing and sales on one side, and operations on the other. The L&N was well aware of tensions that could arise without intent between its departments, and efforts to enhance cooperation led the company, on February 1, 1970, to open a new System Service Center at the Louisville General Office Building. As noted before, the new operation stemmed from the successful regional customer service units already at work in East St. Louis, Memphis, Mobile, and Nashville.

Major goals of the new Center were: to establish and maintain the very best service possible to L&N customers; to provide an adequate supply of freight car equipment to meet the varied needs of shippers; and to achieve maximum utilization and profit from all L&N freight equipment. The Center was also designed to provide at one location information as well as those services which could not come from the local or regional level. In turn, it eliminated much duplication of effort and overlapping of authority which before had divided operating and traffic people on a number of common subjects. The facility also consolidated the Traffic Department's service and car utilization division as well as Operating's car utilization bureau, service bureau and clearance group. Within the Center were these sections:

Clearance section-handled all matters pertaining to clearances, weight restrictions, movement of explosives and other hazardous cargoes. Section staff kept records on all routes as they were cleared, adding newly accumulated data so as to provide latest clearances. The section also maintained data on bridges, cuts and tunnels as well as speed and weight restrictions throughout the system.

"Dependability" became a byword for all CSC staffers and all L&N'ers who dealt with the shipping public. Declared A. R. (Andy) Harkleroad, then Director of Customer Service, "Every car moving on the L&N today is highly competitive. Thus, dependability is what we have to sell to the shipping public. If we can provide such dependability of service through on-time operations, we are delivering our most important product." The system CSC also worked closely with L&N's Operations Center (formerly the Locomotive Utilization Bureau, or LUB), mentioned in Chapter 9.

From "Strawberry to Osborn" at Louisville

Yet another major city terminal was upgraded, this time during the 1970s and in Louisville, hub of L&N routes to Cincinnati, Chicago, Corbin, Evansville-St. Louis, Lexington-Eastern Kentucky and Nashville-Memphis. In its headquarters city, L&N for years relied on two southside yards to classify and make up road trains; several outlying smaller yards also served as collectors and distributors for local industry. One of the train yards, dating from 1905, sat next to the South Louisville Shops, and from World War II years on, it dispatched trains east, north and west. Southward trains were called out of Strawberry Yard, a 1920s-era facility that was enlarged in the 1950s with longer tracks and ramps for automobiles and trailers.

But over time, terminal delays at Louisville began to warrant attention, especially after the 1960s, with the volume of traffic generated by L&N's bigger area shippers, including GE's Appliance Park and the two Ford Motor Company auto and truck assembly plants. Construction on a new hump yard just to the south of old Strawberry Yard got under way in 1973; the hump and "bowl" yard were operational by 1977. The completed yard was officially dedicated in May 1979 and renamed Osborn Yard, after Prime F. Osborn, III, then SCL Industries Chairman and immediate past president of the L&N.

Four miles long and with a 57-track "bowl" or classification yard, Osborn Yard, which was completely automated, was able to classify as many as 4,000 cars per day. Switch foremen of trains being humped worked side by side with yardmasters in the new five—story Yard Tower to remotely handle motive power shoving their cuts. Four computers and related hardware/software maintained yard car inventory and performed certain classifying functions. New one-spot car repair shop, diesel servicing tracks, and improved intermodal handling and storage facilities were also part of improvements made at Osborn.

Family Lines Runthroughs

Advent of the Family Lines System in the 1970s introduced closer coordination with other member roads, bringing about more runthrough train opportunities. Of particular note was a Carolinas-New Orleans service established for a pair of trains originating at Hamlet,

N.C. (on SCL). Those trains, running via Atlanta and an SCL- West Point Route connection, continued on to Montgomery (again over West Point-Western of Alabama trackage) where they were picked up by the L&N for movement south to Mobile and New Orleans.

A faster East- and Gulf-to-West Coast runthrough service also commenced between Jacksonville-New Orleans and Los Angeles; SCL, L&N and Southern Pacific were the participating roads. L&N's Mobile Division (NO&M, M&M, PD and P&A subdivisions) served as "middle man" for that routing and its several runthrough trains, which were to forward a heavy volume of chemical traffic from Texas and Louisiana refineries across the Gulf to the East Coast.

In the important Midwest-Florida intermodal corridor, L&N and SCL further strengthened existing services, continuing the solid

Ron Flanary

Decade of the 1980s marked transition from the Family Lines to, briefly, Seaboard System, then CSX Transportation. Power at this Big Stone, Gap, Va., meet in May 1988 symbolized change. Empty coal train, left, passed Chessie GE units helping tonnage train at right.

Edgar M. Greenwell/L&N Collection/University of Louisville Archives
Solid train of farm machinery left Howell Yard, Evansville, in February 1957 bound for southeastern region farm equipment dealers. F7-GP7-F7 lashup pulled the special.

Chicago-Jacksonville piggyback trains and augmenting them with second sections handling trailers for Atlanta, Nashville and intermediate cities. A Chicago-Waycross run-through freight via Birmingham and SCL's Lineville subdivision was also added. In the final months of its own operation, the L&N began operating freight trains into and from the Belt Railway of Chicago's big Clearing Yard, as well as to and from the Alton & Southern in East St. Louis, Ill.

With the creation of CSX Corporation on November 1, 1980, more changes were made concerning the operation of L&N freight trains: greater coordination between the L&N and C&O-B&O was implemented at Cincinnati, Louisville, Lexington, Ky., and East St. Louis, Ill. For example, the L&N began using the B&O's larger Cone Yard at East St. Louis, while B&O trains left the North Vernon-New Albany, Ind., line to access Louisville via L&N's more direct Short Line from Cincinnati. At Louisville, those trains were shifted from the former K&IT Youngtown Yard to L&N's Osborn Yard.

In Cincinnati, several joint L&N-Chessie trains were scheduled in and out of C&O's new Queensgate Yard at Cincinnati, which by the mid-1980s had supplanted DeCoursey as the principal CSX classification yard for the Cincy gateway. One such joint service was a new Detroit-Birmingham freight train complete with a name, the *Southland Flyer*. Positive philosophical approaches by management matched by sound planning led to the development and implementation of these and other operating improvements, which in turn have helped successors Seaboard System and CSX Transportation build on service strengths so carefully developed by the L&N.

"Extra North 169" was "highballed" through Hubbard Springs, Va., by crew member of Local No. 91, in siding on L&N's Cumberland Valley Division in July 1966.

Sparta Branch local made light work of its consist on this August 1965 day, as GP7 1713 and train crossed Caney Fork River between McMinnville and Sparta, Tenn. The Geep, her caboose and trackage, were all of NC&StL ancestry.

C. Norman Beasley/L&N
Collection/University of
Louisville Archives

Operator of forklift loaded shipment into SAL boxcar at Dixie Cartage, one of industries in Louisville Space Center, warehousing complex next to former Strawberry Yard on south side of Louisville. Company official conferred with L&N sales representative.

L&N Collection/University of
Louisville Archives

Centralized Traffic Control (CTC) also helped greatly to improve freight service. Together with first installation on Birmingham Division in 1942, part of busy "M&M Sub" of MNO&P Division also got CTC during World War II. First trick personnel at Mobile in this 1943 view were, clockwise from top, F. J. Kearley, chief train dispatcher; V. H. Bowen (out of view) and D. L. Laxton, working across from each other; G. A. Merriwether and C. G. Coburn (nearest camera); and Frank Simmons, at then-new CTC console covering Mobile-Flomaton segment.

W.B. Thurman

Diesels were soon to take over, but J-4 Mike 1794 showed her stuff in a dramatic winter farewell as she highballed "First 73" southward down the Louisville Division main stem near Glendale, Ky., in early 1951.

L&N's first piggyback movements were single 31-foot trailers loaded circus-style on 46-foot long modified flatcars. "Tote" trailers at Louisville's Strawberry Yard were ready to roll in August, 1955.

No. 21's Dash to Florida

Picture a starlit summer evening in Chicago with a pleasant breeze blowing in off Lake Michigan. With minor variations, it could be 1968, 1976 or 1981 or even just yesterday! Clock hands inch toward 8:30 p.m., and carmen finish coupling the last air hoses on the trailer flats of L&N's train No. 21, one of two premiere intermodal trains. Road power arrives, and the 37th St. yard crew tacks a caboose on the rear end, then asks the engine crew to set the air for a brake test. With a Florida destination, the solid intermodal train (trailers, containers and auto racks) has but two classifications, "Jack-sonville" and "other Florida TOFC."

Train 21 departs 37th Street right on time, and for the first 14 miles rolls over Chicago & Western Indiana (C&WI) rails. At Dolton Junction, 21 reaches the joint L&N- Missouri Pacific main line and—just beyond—Yard Center, the big freight classification yard shared by the two railroads. There, No. 21 holds the main but collects automobile traffic interchanged from the Grand Trunk Western (which had originated the cars in Michigan). It's a fast pickup, and 21 is rolling again by 9:30 p.m. down the flat, mostly tangent double track main stem to Woodland Junction, Ill. That's where MoPac splits away from L&N, its lines heading toward Southern Illinois,

William C. Tayse/L&N Collection, University of Louisville Archives

With shadows of summer evening in 1967 deepening, hotshot piggybacker No. 21 pulled out of C&EI's 37th Street Yard in Chicago to begin its overnight run to Nashville, Atlanta.

GP30 trio brought No. 721 into downtown Nashville and past historic Union Station, its trainshed and adjacent Kayne Avenue Yard. Nashville stop was brief, only to change crews.

Missouri and the Southwest.

Appearing now as No. 721 on L&N Evansville Division computers and train sheets, the hotshot barrels due south from Woodland Junction at a steady 60 mph, authorized track speed for intermodal trains. Just past midnight, there's a brief crew change at Brewer Yard in Danville, Ill. Then 721 is off and running again.

Ahead lie Terre Haute, Vincennes and Evansville.

Bypassing downtown Evansville on former NYC trackage (which L&N acquired for that purpose), the train arrives at Howell Yard on the city's south side at daybreak.

Thirty minutes are allowed at Howell for a switcher to spot more Florida trailers and racks (from an East St. Louis train) on No. 721's head-end. With the new cars added and a fresh crew aboard, No. 721 is rolling by 6 a.m., crossing over to Henderson, Ky., on L&N's massive three-and-one-half-mile-long Ohio River bridge. "HD" or Henderson Subdivision dispatchers give the hotshot green signals and no delays down their railroad. Next stop for No. 721 is Nashville, reached shortly after 11 a.m. for crew change, inspection and refueling the four diesels. No switching, pickups or setouts were called for at the Music City, a following section (No. 723), handling that traffic.

An 11:30 a.m. departure dispatches the intermodal express down the hillier Chattanooga Subdivision and to the former NC&StL's historic crossing of Cumberland Mountain at Cowan, in Southeastern Tennessee. By then, the train was posted as No. 621

Halfway to Chattanooga, the "pigs" drummed through Decherd, Tn., on former NC&StL mainstem behind U23B team, May, 1981.

on Atlanta Division screens and printouts. A momentary stop is made at Cowan on the north flank of Cumberland for three GP38 helper units based there to couple on. Then, it's up the mountain, through the tunnel and downhill to Sherwood, where the helpers cut off to assist the next northbound. Chattanooga's Wauhatchie Yard is reached at about 3:30 p.m. Again, crews swap, and No. 621 curves by Lookout Mountain, finds bypass trackage around the city to skirt Missionary Ridge, then marches south into Georgia for the final leg of its L&N Land journey.

W&A Subdivision rails lead to Tilford Yard, on Atlanta's northwest side, which No. 621 reaches before 9 p.m., Eastern Time. It's here that the consist is delivered intact to Seaboard Coast Line, which will run the train as No. 321 via Manchester and Waycross, Ga., to Jacksonville. Arrival in the north Florida city, at Moncrief Yard, is scheduled for around 8:30 a.m., making possible second morning delivery for No. 321's racks, containers and trailers to North and Central Florida destinations.

The Chicago-Atlanta route long has been L&N's top growth corridor for intermodal traffic, and No. 21 and its northbound counterpart, No. 20, have ranked as L&N's premiere runs. Their schedules were not particularly fast, as

Wm. C. Tayse/L&N Collection, University of Louisville Archives

No. 21, Chicago-Atlanta-Florida piggyback flyer, ascended approach to Ohio River bridge at Evansville in 1968.

compared with the trailer trains operated by other railroads. Still, considering the hilly Kentucky, Tennessee and Georgia terrain encountered enroute, Nos. 20-21 and sister trains have staged a creditable performance, year after year, thanks to a schedule realistically designed for dependable service rather than speed alone.

Wm. C. Tayse/L&N Collection, University of Louisville Archives

To augment permanant ramps, L&N also used portable ramps for locations offering seasonal or short-term loadings. Tractor-trailer rig backed up portable ramp at Strawberry Yard, Louisville, in September 1964.

J. Parker Lamb

To shorten terminal timings, L&N and C&EI regularly pooled power for Midwest-Southeast piggyback runs. F-units from two roads with No. 21 headed around a reverse curve at Normandy, near Tullahoma, Tenn. in August 1965.

L&N Collection, University of Louisville Archives

So that trilers, auto-racks and other oversized loads could move systemwide, L&N during 1960s enlarged clearances on major routes. Earth-moving machines cleared hillside above restrictive tunnel at Independence, Ky., in summer of 1962.

New Service Called "TOTE"

Intermodal made its debut on the L&N in August, 1955. That's when, with little fanfare, L&N began moving trailers on flatcars between Louisville, Birmingham and New Orleans in the consists of its *Silver Bullet* fast freight trains. Southward, second morning delivery was promised for Birmingham, with third morning delivery at the Crescent City. For the new intermodal operation, L&N bought 30 trailers of three configurations- closed van, open van and flatbed. It meanwhile rebuilt at South Louisville Shops 16 50-ton 24000-series flatcars with new flooring, tire rub rails and aprons or drop plates. Ramps for circus-style loading were built at Strawberry-Louisville, Boyles Yard-Birmingham, and the Julia Street Yard-New Orleans, and local drayers began to handle trailers

No. 22, northbound counterpart of No. 21, curved through the tiny Southern hamlet of Ladds, near Chattanooga. Three SD40s powered the Florida-Atlanta-Chicago TOTE train that May 1981 day.

between ramps and the loading docks of customers.

L&N treated its first intermodal cargoes as simply rail-billed trailerload freight handled at rates competitive with motor carriers. The new service was dubbed Trailer-On-Train-Express, or "TOTE," in good southland vernacular. Early users of TOTE included Paramount Foods, Brown & Williamson Tobacco, General Electric, U.S. Steel, American Sugar Refining and National Gypsum. Some months behind other Midwestern roads to introduce piggyback, L&N became the first in the Central South offering the new mode.

From its start, TOTE was a rousing success; shippers liked the convenience of load-dock to load-dock service, coupled with fast in-transit schedules. Within a year, Cincinnati-Atlanta and St. Louis-Nashville-Birmingham TOTE

routes were added, with Evansville and Memphis coming on line in 1958. More flat cars joined the fleet that year, and L&N arranged with both C&EI and Monon to forward trailers to Chicago, from Evansville and Louisville, respectively. In 1959 L&N joined the recently formed Trailer-Train Corporation to take advantage of TTX's far larger pool of standardized flatcars, many providing a 75-foot length to accommodate not one but two trailers. The linkup was advantageous to both supplier and carrier. L&N transported some 2,000 trailers that year.

Until 1962, almost all L&N trailer traffic rolled in consists of regularly scheduled fast freights, but that year, the road sought to improve timing of some TOTE services by adding trailers to consists of passenger trains. A new Louisville-Memphis TOTE service benefitted from trailers moving south of Bowling Green, Ky., on overnight Memphis Line passenger trains No.101-4. Mainline fast freights worked the trailers between Louisville and Bowling Green. But, it was the Memphis Line "varnish" which brought about a 24- hour overall speedup of the Louisville- Memphis TOTE service.

A similar operation utilizing Nos. 17-18, the *Flamingo*, saved 12 hours on the Cincinnati - Atlanta run, with trailers added at Knoxville, or switched out, depending upon direction. For a time, the *Pan American* hustled Gulf Coast-bound trailers south of Nashville, while the

northbound *Azalean* moved trailers between Nashville, Louisville and Cincinnati. The back-up move into Union Station, Louisville, necessitated a yard switcher holding out the TOTES while No. 4's consist was worked under the trainshed.

The number of points served by L&N TOTE services also grew steadily. Starting with just three cities in 1955, L&N by 1962 had expanded TOFC service to 29 cities. TOTE trailers by then ranged off-line, to Chicago, Denver, Houston, Kansas City and Minneapolis. By 1970, L&N piggyback was systemwide, with 68 permanent and 15 portable-ramp points.

Wm. C. Tayse/L&N Collection, University of Louisville Archives

After improving clearances in 1960s, L&N worked some intermodal traffic in consists of regularly scheduled fast freights. Trailers and auto-racks brought up the rear of Short Line fast freight at Independence , Ky., on its way to Louisville in 1967.

Automobile Transport, TOTE Expand

Another facet of Intermodal—the movement of new automobiles and trucks—experienced great growth in those same years. That service began in the late 1950s, when L&N tested several conventional over-the-road auto carriers as piggyback shipments. The tests proved successful, but with the advent of 85- and 89-foot long multi-level rack cars by 1959, L&N soon after took advantage of the higher capacity and resulting lower rates the racks could offer. The road also began to expand such shipments across the system, at the same time launching an extensive clearance program to open up—or, in some cases, eliminate altogether—restrictive tunnels, especially in Kentucky and Tennessee. All of the above led

During 1960s, L&N also tried handling trailers on the rear of passenger trains. A carman coupled air hoses at Nashville Union Station, as trailers were added to the southbound *Pan American* in August 1965.

L&N Collection, University of Louisville Archives

Big auto-handling facilities at Nashville's Radnor Yard and other on-line cities, were equipped with moveable ramps to load, unload vehicles faster.

rather logically to the concentration of heavier automotive and piggyback movements as solid trains, again, to meet the great growth of those new traffic sources on the L&N.

In 1962, the L&N and C&EI inaugurated a fast new all-TOTE train between Chicago and Atlanta. That train, operating as the second section of No. 95, the fabled *Dixie Flyer*, became the forerunner of the later quartet of all-trailer-trains, Nos. 20-23, in the Chicago-Nashville-Atlanta corridor. "Second 95," as the train was designated, offered a 24-hour service between the Great Lakes and the Georgia Capitol, fastest ever for any joint C&EI-L&N freight schedule up till then. Initial consists of a dozen or less flatcars grew solidly into 40- to 45-car train loads. Leading national freight forwarders along with big Midwestern mail order houses became regular users of 2/95 and sister trains.

Experiencing parallel growth in its automotive traffic, L&N by the early 1960s began concentrating new auto-rack traffic on a separate Nashville-Atlanta train, No. 55. A Louisville connection fed traffic to No. 55. As an interesting sidelight for this development, the New York Central at about the same time began routing via its Louisville branch trainloads of new Michigan—assembled autos destined for points beyond Louisville. At Strawberry Yard, Louisville, L&N combined the NYC-originating racks with loads from a big local Ford Motor Co., plant, running both cuts to Nashville as one solid train. Some of that traffic continued on to Atlanta in No. 55's consist. For its booming automotive traffic, L&N built new ramps and vehicle-storage terminals in Louisville, Nashville, Birmingham, Atlanta and New Orleans.

Other ways were also explored to promote and help intermodal services grow. In 1964, L&N tried utilizing piggyback for less than car-load (LCL) services. Agreements were made with various local trucking companies to perform pick up and delivery services, and interline LCL service (via piggyback) was arranged with Atlantic Coast Line, Missouri Pacific, C&EI, Great Northern, MoPac and Soo Line. For a time, TOFC helped to reverse the decline in LCL shipments, and a contemporary internal report on the efficiency of the service credited 300 trailer trips as having replaced 900 box car trips.

L&N also joined Fruit Growers Express to utilize the fleet of refrigerated trailers the second carrier offered, and the railroad sold its own original trailer fleet to REA Leasing Corporation (REALCO) to be able to lease trailers from that company's much larger national trailer pool. And, beginning in the 60s, the U.S. Postal Department began entrusting trailerloads of U.S. Mail to L&N and other railroads.

Second Sections, Bigger Terminals

More trains, meanwhile, went into service, helping L&N move the growing volume of intermodal traffic, which, just in the piggyback category, amounted to well over 65,000 trailers by 1965. As previously noted, a second pair of trains were added in the Chicago-Atlanta corri-

L&N Collection, University of Louisville Archives

At New Orleans, L&N placed its auto ramp at Gentilly Yard on the industrial east side of the city. Engine terminal, south end of train yard were at upper left.

dor; Nos. 2/94-5 were renumbered 20-21 and eventually extended to Jacksonville, with SCL's participation south of Atlanta. Scheduled fast freights between East St. Louis and Evansville added more intermodal traffic to those trains.

In the Cincinnati-Atlanta corridor, two new trains, Nos. 44-45 and named the *Autovans*, went into operation to expedite Midwest—Southeast automotive and trailer movements. Some of that traffic, destined for Florida, was combined with No. 21's consist at Tilford Yard in Atlanta. Between Cincinnati and Birmingham, yet another combined auto-pig train came on in the later 1960s. At Nashville, it picked up cars from Chicago, Evansville and St. Louis. As with most of its intermodal trains, L&N endeavored to pre-block cars at originating ramps or yards to eliminate or reduce switching at intermediate points.

To better accommodate its growing container and trailer traffic, L&N also significantly expanded its piggyback terminals. Circus-style loading, performed in the months just after 1955, gave way to more flexible mobile gantry cranes and side-lift trucks, which were pur-

chased to transfer trailers and containers at the enlarged ramps in Atlanta, Chicago, Cincinnati, East St. Louis and Nashville (at the last named city, a new intermodal terminal opened in 1984). Eventually, the number of individual ramps around the system was scaled back somewhat, as the L&N—and later Seaboard System and CSX Transportation—began to concentrate intermodal loadings at strategically located hub terminals across the system. Automobile- and truck-handling facilities also came in for expansion and upgrading during the 1960s and 1970s.

Intermodal traffic continued to grow steadily on the L&N. By 1970, the road was handling over 124,000 containers and trailers and nearly 50,000 carloads of new autos and trucks each year. As traffic folk became fond of saying, L&N's pigs had indeed gone to market! Today, the modern CSX Transportation, L&N's successor, continues to build on that intermodal legacy and stands in the best possible position to garner Midwest-Southeastern traffic with single-line service that competitors will be hard put to match.

In June 1954, M-1 1962 led a long train of empty opentops out of DeCoursey Yard on their way back to eastern Kentucky mines. The Cincy and EK Divisions were steam's last stronghold on the L&N.

Heavy Coal Hauler

A Tradition of Bituminous— A Brief History of Coal on the L&N

The L&N long ranked itself as one of the nation's major coal hauling railroads. From the early 1900s on, a major share of its annual revenues was derived from bituminous coal traffic that originated in five distinct geographic regions. Early on, the stage was set for that traffic dominance, not only as the road pushed its tracks into the Eastern Kentucky coal country after 1865 but also in other developments even as its first trains began to roll between Louisville and Nashville.

Old corporate records indicate that probably L&N's first coal traffic of any consequence was so-called "river coal," en route from Pennsylvania mines to Ohio Valley cities and thence into the interior of Kentucky. Very early in its existence, the road garnered some

of that traffic, distributing it to communities along the main line. According to those records, first mention of coal traffic other than the "river coals" noted movement in 1866 of eleven cars of coal that originated, oddly enough, in Hart and Warren Counties, which had not been recognized up till then as Kentucky "coal" counties. However, three years later, in 1869, several shipments of coal were loaded in Rockcastle County, on the outer fringe of an emerging coal-producing region in Eastern Kentucky. Those shipments, incidentally, moved toward Louisville over L&N's Lebanon Branch, which had just been completed into Rockcastle County.

Before 1870, the L&N burned wood almost exclusively in the fireboxes of its locomotives. But that year the company, using coal from recently opened mines in the Western Kentucky coal fields, tested the fuel in several locomotives. Not only was the fuel cheaper

L&N Collection, University of Louisville Archives

The Western Kentucky coal fields became productive several decades earlier than did fields in the eastern part of the state. With several loaded L&N wood gons at left, the South Diamond Mine and Tipple near Madisonville were pictured about 1912.

First FULL Train of coal From a HAZARD mine APR. 1915 From KY. JEWEL COAL CO 33 cars BLOCK COAL

L&N Collection, University of Louisville Archives

In April 1915, the first solid train of coal from a Hazard-area mine was ready to roll north behind H-18 class 2-8-0 913. The 33 gons and hoppers of block coal had just been loaded by the Kentucky Jewel Coal Company.

but also it improved performance of the engines tested. Thereafter, all orders for new locomotives specified that they be constructed to burn coal, and engines already in service began to be converted to the newer fuel. Thus L&N became a major consumer of coal as well as a transporter

The year 1871 was an important one in the development of L&N's coal traffic base. It was then that the Nashville & Decatur Railroad was acquired (by lease), opening up a through route into Northern Alabama and moving the Old Reliable that much closer to what soon became the great major coal mining and steel-producing district surrounding Birmingham. Meanwhile, the South & North Alabama Railroad had built northward from Montgomery but could not muster the neces-

sary capital to finish the gap between Calera and Decatur. Through acquisition of the S&NA, again by lease, the L&N finished the line, a feat that was accomplished in September 1872. As is now well known, the intersection of the S&NA and a Norfolk Southern predecessor at a tiny hamlet called Elyton in Jefferson County, Ala., led to the rise of the great city of Birmimgham. L&N subsequently invested heavily in building a network of tracks to reach area mines and other mineral resources, inasmuch as a share of the Alabama coal went locally to the production of iron and, later, steel.

The Western Kentucky coal fields, which embraced all or part of some 14 counties, began to generate a growing volume of traffic from its mines during the 1870s, and in 1879-

80, with purchase of the St. Louis & Southeastern's Kentucky Division (which ran squarely through the district), L&N was able to secure more coal traffic. New branches and feeder lines were also constructed to better serve that district. While its mines were never to achieve the prominence of their eastern Kentucky counterparts, nonetheless they contained several millions of tons of recoverable reserves and for many decades produced sizeable traffic volumes for the L&N, as did coal producing areas in Southern Illinois and Indiana. The higher sulphur content of Western Kentucky coal would not become a negative factor until recent years.

With growth in coal traffic from the Alabama and Western Kentucky districts, the L&N developed both domestic and export markets for its expanding coal traffic.

Two ocean-going steamers, the *August Belmont* and *E. O. Saltmarsh*, were acquired in 1895 to handle coal to Latin American ports and across the Atlantic to Western Europe. The ships continued to haul coal for the railroad until the subsidiary which owned them was sold in 1915. Largely on the strength of Alabama coal fields production, total coal traffic on the L&N reached 4.6 million tons by the turn of the century.

Eastern Kentucky Coal

As early as the Civil War, L&N officers were well aware of the vast coal resources which lay in the Cumberland Plateau region of Eastern Kentucky, East Tennessee and Southwestern Virginia. Interest in that region in fact motivated extension of L&N's Lebanon Branch toward the region from 1865 on. By 1882-3, L&N had pushed the branch beyond Rockcastle County (and a temporary terminus at Livingston, Ky., during the 1870s) and on to the Tennessee state line at Jellico to enter the mining district centered about that community. The advent of greatly improved transport spurred more development in the Jellico District, and by 1889 contracts had been signed with some 10 mines between Jellico and London (Ky.) to ship their coal north by rail to Louisville.

Extension of the Lebanon Branch during the early 1880s also made it possible for the L&N to eventually reach the rich coal fields in Bell and Harlan County, although the necessary work occurred in several stages and took place over a span of 20 or more years. Initial construction of what was to become L&N's Cumberland Valley Division got underway in the late 1880s, when the road pushed a line southeastward from Corbin to Middlesbo-

The crew of The First Creek Branch mine run stood for its portrait at Harveyton, in Perry County, Ky., one of the earlier tipples along the Eastern Kentucky Division. In this 1915 view, H-6 2-8-0 713 led an auxiliary tender, possibly because not all EK water tanks had been constructed by then.

The hogger of "Big Emma" 1953 "had 'em in the wind" as his northbound coal train sped along the double track CV Division toward Corbin in September 1955. This scenic Cumberland River locale near Artemus, Ky., was a favorite for L&N photographers over the years.

rough and Norton, Va. Then, between 1909-10, a diverging line was built from Harbell, near Pineville, up the Cumberland River Valley and into Harlan County to reach the towns of Harlan and Benham. That construction, along with several feeder branches, resulted in the first load of Harlan County coal being shipped from the Aldrian Mine of the former Wallins Creek Coal Company on August 25, 1911.

Meanwhile farther to the north, two other railroads were being constructed along or near the North Fork of the Kentucky River in the direction of the Hazard and Elkhorn Region coal fields. These lines were later to form much of L&N's Eastern Kentucky Division. First was the Lexington & Eastern, which had built eastward from its Bluegrass city terminus during the 1880s to reach Jackson, in Breathitt

R. L. Kirkpatrick/L&N Collection, University of Louisville Archives

After stopping for water at the south end of the Red River bridge, booster-equipped J-4A Mike 1903 had a northbound coal train rolling upgrade to Winchester and Cincinnati. The 233-foot high trestle, on the EK Division between Ravenna-Winchester, was L&N's tallest. Out of sight, another 2-8-2 shoved hard against the wooden caboose on the train's rear.

County by 1891. Second was the Louisville & Atlantic which, having consolidated with several previously built lines, by 1912 operated a through route from Frankfort to Beattyville, just west of Jackson.

In 1909-10, the L&N acquired both the L&E and the L&A, then went on to lay another 100 miles of track up the North Fork of the Kentucky to Hazard and Whitesburg. The newly completed Eastern Kentucky Division's "North Fork Extension" generated its first revenue load of coal on October 5, 1912, a 40-ton car consigned from the old Speaks Coal Company tipple to a manufacturer at Clay City, Ky., on the former L&E. Then, in April 1915, the railroad operated its first solid train of coal from the Hazard fields. By 1916 coal traffic had grown to 15.5 million tons, a 237 percent increase over 1900. By 1922, L&N was moving upwards of 22 million tons of coal annually.

Coal's Roaring Twenties, the Depression, and the War Years

Major capital investments were made in the Eastern Kentucky coal fields in the early years of the 1920s. New yards were built at Ravenna on the EK Division and at Loyall, near Harlan, on the CV Division. A new roundhouse, car and locomotive shop and servicing facilities were also built at Corbin and the yard expanded there. And, double track was installed on the Kentucky Division between Corbin and Winchester, the Cumberland Valley Division between Corbin and Harlan Junction, and at strategic locations on the Eastern Kentucky Division (a decade earlier, double track went in between Athens and Calera, Ala., to greatly improve train operations on the vital Birmingham Division main trunk).

In 1927, a 750-ton per hour coaling plant at

L&N Collection, University of Louisville Archives
A northbound unit train on the Cincinnati Division's "KY" main trunk approached Grants Tunnel just south of DeCoursey Yard. "Class" FA2 300 led a sister Alco cab on the solid train of coal, destined for Midwestern markets north of Cincy.

A typical mid-20th century coalfield scene in Harlan County, Ky., revealed L&N hoppers being loaded with various sizes of coal—block, lump, egg and nut. "Fines," or slack coal as mine operators called them, were dumped in the hoppers, at left. The unit train was not yet in L&N's vocabulary.

Pensacola (on the Gulf Coast) was opened to load export coal into ocean ships; the plant replaced an older loading pier the L&N had erected in the 1880s. In 1927, L&N's total coal traffic peaked at 42.1 million tons, a record that would not be eclipsed until 1970. During the deepest part of the Great Depression, L&N's coal traffic plummeted from the 1927 high (42.1 million tons) to 19.6 million tons in 1932.

Fortunately, traffic would again rise as the decade wore on and as economic conditions improved. The World War II years which followed brought increased tonnage as the nation embraced the enormous task of defeating the Axis powers.

During and just after the war, the L&N built more branch lines into the coal fields, notably the Leatherwood Creek Branch in 1945 (EK), the Clover Fork Extension in 1947 (CV) and the Rockhouse Creek Branch (also EK) in 1949. Brand new yards were also opened at Dent and Crawford on the EK in 1949. Coal traffic reached a post-war high of 38.1 million tons in 1948, only to fall to 25.4 million tons in 1950 as a result of market declines and coal industry labor disruptions. Still, King Coal continued to reign as L&N's top commodity, contributing some 31 per cent of all revenue dollars and generating a good 44 per cent of all freight tonnages.

The Glenbrook mine and coal washing plant, then operated by the Stonega Coal & Coke Co., sat at the far eastern end of L&N's Clover Fork Branch (CV Division). Red L&N hoppers were spotted for loading, in this December 1961 view.

The "Modern" Coal Era Begins

The two decades of the 1950s and '60s were transitional ones for coal, as markets changed from domestic and industrial use to utility growth, particularly in the South. L&N ordered new hopper cars for its fleet, maintaining its claim to owning one of the youngest car fleets in the nation. After 1957 coal ceased to be a fuel for L&N's locomotive fleet, as L&N accomplished its program of complete dieselization early that year. A new marshalling yard at Atkinson, Ky. (near Madisonville), was opened in 1963 to serve an increase in coal traffic from the western Kentucky fields.

With the NC&StL merger in 1957, the L&N inherited additional coal traffic from Southeastern Tennessee. Most of that coal, of coking grade and ideal for industrial use, was mined and loaded along two branches that ventured north from the former NC&StL main line at Cowan, Tn. (the Tracy City Branch), and Bridgeport, Ala. (the Sequatchie Valley Branch). However, loadings from the two branches produced far less volume as compared to the higher production districts on the L&N proper. The Tracy City Branch was later abandoned, while the Sequatchie Valley Branch was sold to a regional rail operator in the 1980s. For a ten year period after 1955, L&N coal traffic remained mostly stable.

Annual tonnages fluctuated from about 34 to 38 million tons, making up about 40% of the railroad's total traffic mix. But, beginning in 1965, traffic began to grow as new steam-powered electric generating plants came on line across the South.

Observing a restricted speed track order, CV Division local No. 64 eased through Big Stone Gap, Va., behind RS3 132 in summer 1954. The "south end" of the CV handled coal routed via the N&W/ Norton, as well as coal for markets in the Carolinas via the Clinchfield and ACL/SAL connections at CRR's south end.

Knowledgeable parties also foresaw an energy crisis on the horizon; meanwhile, coal had become more competitive with crude oil, natural gas and other petroleum products. By 1970, system loadings reached 48.1 million tons, an all-time high for the L&N.

Even during the years of depressed loadings, coal train movements were substantial. For example, on the busy Cumberland Valley Division between Corbin and Loyall, dispatchers scheduled seven or more daily northbound coal trains, with a corresponding number of empty hopper runs southward. At Corbin, single cars of coal were classified for movement either north to Cincinnati or south to Knoxville. Unit trains (then being introduced) were not classified; their consists were merely yarded for crew change and refueling power. Main line trains out of Loyall and north and south from Corbin handled from 70 to 100 cars of coal. Similar operating patterns could be found on other L&N coal-hauling routes in Western Kentucky and Alabama.

From Single Cars to Unit Trains

With the early 1960s came new developments in coal hopper cars and introduction of integral or "unit" trains, solid coal runs that loaded in motion at minesites, highballed to users, then unloaded to return promptly to the minefields. In 1962 the L&N began developing three different prototype 100-ton capacity cars for unit train service, and the selected design was duplicated in quantity at L&N's South Louisville Shops. The finished cars (which were painted orange) were then placed in unit train service in a Paradise, Ky., to Widow's Creek, Ala., cycle. Conventional discharge 100-ton hoppers also entered service in 1964 on the "Steel Train." This movement, on L&N's CV Division, involved a twice daily operation between Corbin and U.S. Steel Corporation's mines at Lynch, Ky.

The assigned 100-car trains loaded coal from mines at Lynch, then proceeded to the steel company's washing plant at Corbin, with 10,000 tons being delivered daily. After processing, the washed coal was reloaded into the same hoppers and shipped north each night up the "KY" Subdivision to the Cincinnati gateway. From Cincy, either the New York Central or the Pennsylvania forwarded the trains on to U.S. Steel's Gary, Ind., mills. In common with the rapid discharge cars, the new unit train cars were painted bright orange with white reflective lettering. L&N wanted distinctive equipment to showcase this new era of coal transportation. The car fleet, however, was still dominated by 50-, 60- and 70-ton cars; only 3.4 percent of L&N's 33,459 coal hoppers in 1965 were of 100-ton capacity.

One of L&N's first unit coal train operations was the previously mentioned run between the Peabody Coal Company's mine at Paradise, Ky., and Tennessee Valley Authority's steam generating plant at Widow's Creek, Ala., near Bridgeport (on the Nashville-Atlanta main line). Initially, 5,000 tons of coal were loaded each day from a conveyor belt system into a 64-car train traversing a track loop; loading took about two hours and 30 minutes. At Widow's Creek, the arriving train was rotary-dumped, and the empties returned to Paradise for reloading the next day. The 425-mile round trip took less than 48 hours—including loading, dumping, and inspections.

Other early unit train movements on the L&N included the Cumberland Valley Division's Merna and Amru to Plant McDonough, Ga., trains. These 84-car runs loaded at CV mines on the Martin's Fork Branch (at Merna) south of Loyall on the Yellow Creek Branch (at Amru) near Pineville for transit via the Knoxville & Atlanta Division to Georgia Power's McDonough steam plant near Cartersville, Ga. Starting in 1966, the Bull Run train, another early movement, loaded at various mines on the Eastern Kentucky Division and proceeded to TVA's then-new Bull Run steam plant near Oak Ridge, Tn. The Bull Run service used 100-ton L&N designed and built rapid discharge hoppers.

Ron Flanary

On August 3, 1967, "Extra 1413," a northbound EK Subdivision coal train, blasted through Jackson, Ky. for the climb up Elkatawa Hill. Two Alco Centuries were the road power. Helper power for the same train is pictured on page 163.

Ron Flanary

RS-3 158 wrestled loads and empties in the south end of the North Hazard, Ky., yard on August 3, 1967. The small terminal occasionally got chocked full of open tops, loaded and empty, a situation that appeared to have been the case that August day.

The Market Shift Grows

As the L&N entered its final full decade (1970s) of corporate existence, it was handling well over 700,000 carloads of coal annually. That converted into some 60 million tons of coal. Directly served were over 250 active mines in six geographic regions. The big volume producers remained the Eastern Kentucky and Southeastern Kentucky fields. Other fields included Eastern Tennessee, near Jellico (between Corbin and Knoxville), Northern Alabama, Western Kentucky, and Southern Illinois/Indiana. Most L&N coal traffic moved from mines to public utility plants, steel mills, and other industries or to rail/water transfer points for domestic and export usage. Export coal flowed to Mobile and Norfolk, Va., while domestic rail/water shipments went to Chicago on Lake Michigan, or to Ohio River transfer facilities near Cincinnati, Evansville, Louisville, and Carrollton, Ky.

For most of the L&N's history, "King Coal" moved predominantly northward from yards at Corbin, Hazard, Loyall and Ravenna to Cincinnati and Louisville gateways. There, connecting roads—B&O, NYC, Monon and Pennsy—handled the coal on to Midwestern or Northeastern consignees. A fair amount of L&N coal also went north to the Great Lakes on the C&O via its Northern Division through Columbus, Ohio. But, with the industrialization of the Sunbelt in the Post World War II decades and the corresponding growth of utilities to provide power to match that growth, the demand in southern States after 1965 for coal became urgent. By the early 1970s, that demand, coupled with the energy crisis, was to

W. C. Tayse/L&N Collection,
University of Louisville
Archives

"Extra 1537 South" eased its train of 70 empty 100-ton hoppers through Cimarron Coal's fast-loading tipple near Madisonville, Ky., in December 1971. Never stopping, the train filled up with coal, then hustled south to Georgia Power Co.'s Plant Bowen near Cartersville.

profoundly affect L&N's coal traffic patterns.

During the 1970s, L&N continued to roll significant coal tonnages from Eastern Kentucky origins north to Cincinnati as well as from Western Kentucky/Southern Indiana points toward Chicago on former C&EI and Monon routes. Coal also continued to roll to the steel mills in the Birmingham area, also to Mobile for export loadings. However, new coal traffic moving through the Atlanta gateway to utilities in southeastern states came close to overwhelming the road. By the end of the decade, L&N coal department men calculated that their traffic had increased 60 percent in ten short years.

The problems were felt the greatest on the eastern side of the system, namely, on the EK and CV Subdivisions and on the Cincinnati to Atlanta main line.

By the mid 1970s, northbound tonnage in the Cincy-Atlanta corridor had increased 28%, while southbound tonnage, much of which had to traverse the mountainous single-track Knoxville Subdivision south of Corbin, jumped an enormous 148%. The Atlanta Division's Cartersville-Tilford Yard segment may well have experienced the greatest burden, funneling traffic off both the Corbin-Knoxville and the Nashville-Chattanooga main lines. For a

railroad built primarily to haul coal to factories of the Midwest and North, the new traffic patterns of the 1960s and '70s created serious car and motive power shortages and in time exacted a terrible toll on L&N's physical plant.

Contributing to the L&N's dilemma were two severely cold winters, in 1976-77 and in 1977-78, also a four-month miners' strike in early 1978. Those events conspired to greatly strain the railroad's open top hopper car supply. During the two extreme winter seasons, frozen or unthawed coal kept cars in the north for much longer periods than normal. But then, after the '78 strike was settled, over-production by the mines dumped yet more coal on the L&N, much more than it could safely handle.

Also impacting the situation were low coal rates and an archaic system for car orders at mine tipples. By the late 1970s, low coal rates, instituted years before for northern industries and utilities, failed to yield revenues the L&N needed to expand its car and locomotive fleet and make track and terminal improvements. And too, railroad and mines continued to follow an inefficient, outdated rating system that greatly inflated the actual number of cars required for a particular day of loading.

Several steps led to L&N's recovery. One

R. D. Acton, Sr.

Helper service over Duff Mountain was re-established by the L&N in 1978 to expedite running times of loaded southbound coal trains between Corbin and Atlanta better motive power utilization was also a major objective. Two GE U-25Cs pushed a tonnage train over Davis Creek Trestle just south of Habersham, Tenn., in October 1979. For some inexplicable reason, the train had two cabooses, one lettered for L&N, the other for SCL.

Ron Flanary

Behind "Extra 1413's" caboose ,(from page 160) three wide-open F-units kept the slack bunched, as "EK" coal moved north in August,

Brad McClelland
An EK mine run loaded coal at Lost Mining's tipple at Bulan, Ky. on the EK Subdivision. Three Alco C-420's handled the train that day, October 11, 1980.

was realignment in 1976 of the several coal-originating divisions on the east side of the system. That year, the CV, EK and certain mainline segments of the Cincinnati and Knoxville Divisions came together as the new Corbin Division, headquartered at Corbin, Ky.

Installation in the new division office building of computer-assisted dispatching and centralized traffic control followed, in 1977. To give the road the motive power it badly needed for the increased coal traffic, the Interstate Commerce Commission in September 1978 ordered corporate parent Seaboard Coast Line to supply 100 locomotive units. In the months preceding, L&N had leased power from any carrier or company that could spare it—

notably Conrail, DT&I, Canadian National, N&W, SP and Precision National.

Then in 1979, the ICC granted the L&N a 22 per cent rate increase on interstate coal movements and a smaller increase on intrastate movements, both of which the road had applied for the year before. L&N's rate requests were coupled to a nationwide increase also authorized by the commission. Buoyed by the new revenues, the railroad commenced a $427-million capital improvement program to purchase new open top hopper cars and locomotives. It used the monies to also enlarge yards at Corbin, Etowah, Ravenna and other intermediate coal-handling terminals, build new second track at key "chock" points on

The Shamrock Coal Company operated its own motive power, bathtub gondolas and even cabooses. In distinctive cream-green colors, the trains ran under the "Oneida & Western" name. In February, 1987, an "O&W" unit coal train prepared to leave the Corbin, Ky., yard.

main coal routes in Kentucky and Tennessee and otherwise undertake extraordinary maintenance on the battered coalfield lines.

The more frequent use by the late 1970s of coal company or utility-owned hopper car fleets also helped greatly to ease L&N's problems. Lucrative rate incentives were offered companies if they provided their own equipment. That also guaranteed a steady car supply as opposed to sole reliance on railroad-owned hoppers. Eastern Kentucky coal operators South-East Coal, and Shamrock Coal went one step beyond, purchasing locomotives built to L&N specs to handle their traffic. Although those firms owned the equipment from front coupler to rear, L&N continued to provide crews and to operate those trains.

The era of the local mine run was not over just yet. By then, L&N's coal traffic moved in all directions, not only by the train load, but also in smaller blocks and even single car-loads. Traffic was interchanged with the Clinchfield, Georgia, Seaboard Coast Line and Southern Railway for movement to East Coast, Central South and Southeastern destinations. Export coal moved also to the Gulf Coast and to Norfolk, the latter via the N&W.

Northbound coal was regularly transloaded to boats on Lake Michigan at Chicago, as well as interchanged with the Elgin, Joliet & Eastern and other lines for delivery to northern Illinois, Indiana and Wisconsin area steel mills and power generating plants.

The Coal Commitment

The L&N and coal were synonymous. Although the character of the railroad differed from one division to the next, most folk would acknowledge the prominent place of coal in L&N's traffic base, no matter where one watched one of its train go by. The company was long dedicated to the coal standard and backed that commitment with equipment, facilities and extensive research to assist its coal shippers in reaching maximum utilization. With the Old Reliable's passage into corporate history, successors Seaboard System and CSX Transportation have continued to build upon the great coal-handling achievements attained by the L&N Railroad.

William McMurry "oiled around" his K-4B Pacific at Nashville's Union Station just before taking the *Pan-American* to Birmingham on a summer afternoon in the late 1930s. McMurry and several other L&N enginemen became well known to regional radio audiences as result of WSM broadcasts of the "Pan" as it roared south from Nashville.

Power for the Pull: L&N's Motive Power

R ailroad observers often focus more attention on motive power, since the locomotive itself is the most visually exciting part of a moving train. This chapter, while not necessarily a detailed treatise on motive power, attempts nonetheless to survey the development of the locomotives that pulled the Old Reliable's trains.

L&N motive power history closely follows the road's corporate philosophy: conservative. Generally speaking, L&N steam locomotives were of moderate size and capacity, tailored for specific services. Large 10-coupled or articulated engines never found their way onto the roster; heavy 2-8-2 Mikado and 2-8-4 Berkshire types were the biggest steam power owned by L&N. Excepting two three-cylinder engines bought in the 1920s, Old Reliable's mechanical men shied away from experimentals as well as excessive gadgetry, relying instead on proven types and designs. The same thinking carried forward into dieseldom; while L&N early on did spread orders for new units among the several builders, it again relied on basic "off the shelf" models, for example, six-axle units for passenger, four-axle cabs and boosters for freight, along with road-switchers for locals, mine runs and mixed duties, and, later, higher horsepowered six-axle hoods for coal trains and tonnage freights.

1850 to 1900

At the outset, the L&N was proposed as a six-foot gauge pike running between its namesake cities. Accordingly, the new road ordered three 4-4-0 steam locomotives of the wide gauge from the Kentucky Locomotive Works, located in Louisville. However, by 1855, with just a few miles of track having been laid, management decided to change track gauge to the more common five foot width then used by most other railroads in the south. Little else is known about the wide-footed Americans, which were thought to have been sold to other railroads.

By late 1859, after regular trains commenced running from Louisville to Nashville, the roster included some 20 4-4-0s as well as several 0-6-0 and 0-8-0 engines for switching and Muldraugh Hill pusher service. Needing a major back shop to maintain its rolling stock, L&N the previous year purchased the Kentucky Locomotive Works, which was given the added responsibility of producing new power. American (4-4-0) no. 30 was the first L&N-built engine to roll out of the "new" shop in 1860. Also that year, the road bought (from Baldwin) its first 2-6-0 or Mogul-type freight locomotive. At the end of 1860, 38 locomotives were in service.

L&N Collection
University of Louisville Archives
L&N's original no. 8, the "Davidson," was built by Baldwin in 1858, one year before the first train ran through from Louisville to Nashville. Pictured at Louisville in 1880, the engine served for some years as a Muldraugh Hill helper.

L&N Collection/University of Louisville Archives

Buildings of the former Kentucky Locomotive Works in Louisville were acquired in 1858 by the L&N for its first shop complex. In an early 1870s view, two 4-4-0s under steam waited for their runs, while employees "decorated" the tops of what appeared to be early cabooses.

After the Civil War, the L&N hired a talented locomotive designer, Thatcher Perkins, from the Baltimore & Ohio. Perkins previously had directed that company's motive power development. Under Perkins' hand, the L&N began turning out low wheeled 4-4-0 types as well as a group of large 4-6-0s. The ten-wheelers, four of which had been "upgraded" from earlier Moguls, weighed over 45 tons each, monsters compared the original 4-4-0s. It was also during this time that Perkins turned his attention to designs for a large 2-6-0 or Mogul, the type becoming L&N's mainline heavy freight engine during the 1870s. While some of the Moguls were built at Louisville, most were turned out by the Baldwin and Rogers Locomotive Works. It was also under Perkins' hand that the road converted its locomotives from wood to coal burners.

With the decades of the 1880s and 90s came yet heavier, larger power, the 2-8-0 or Consolidation type, to take over as the standard freight hauler for Old Reliable. The first engines of that wheel arrangement, four in number, were built in 1883-4 under the direction of Reuben Wells, Mr. Perkins' successor, at the Louisville Shops. Another 31 such engines

followed over the next three years from the Rogers Company. In the following 10 years, the L&N was to acquire more than 150 2-8-0s, which were produced by various builders as well as by the Louisville Shops. Beginning in the early 1890s, the road also bought larger 4-6-0 or Ten-Wheelers, to power its major passenger trains. By then, those two principal locomotive types—2-8-0 and 4-6-0—were to power the L&N into the new century.

Steaming into the Twentieth Century

By 1900, L&N's system expansion had far outpaced capacity of the old 10th and Kentucky Shops in Louisville. In 1902, construction began on the huge new shops at South Louisville. It was at the 70-acre, 35-building complex, which opened in 1905, that L&N centered all major car and locomotive repair work. And, it was there that the road continued its tradition of building many new locomotives, the plant alone producing 400 engines from 1905 through 1923, 282 of them to L&N's own designs.

After 1900, the L&N accelerated purchase of 2-8-0 freight locomotives by adding 300 more to the active roster. From 1905 to 1911,

L&N Collection/University of Louisville Archives

Straight boilered No. 74 was built by Baldwin in 1870 and was shown shortly after delivery. Later rebuilt at Louisville, the engine ran well beyond 1900, although one doubts if its ornate livery lasted quite that long!

the well designed H-23, and two improved versions, the H-25 and H-27, became the standard freight haulers for the road. Constructed by Baldwin, Rogers and South Louisville, the engines shared some specs, such as 57" drivers, but weights ranged from 183,400 to 196,000 pounds for the three classes. The newer H-25s and H-27s were equipped with superheaters, piston valves and Walchaert valve gears.

Although freight power may have claimed center stage, passenger power was not being ignored. Rogers delivered five 4-6-2 or Pacific types in 1905, L&N's first steam power with a trailing truck under the firebox. Quite pleased with the performance from its new K-1 class "varnish" haulers, the road built 20 more in its new South Louisville Shops. Another 20 Pacifics, an improved version classed as K-2s, were turned out by the Louisville shops, beginning in 1909.

Between 1911-1923, South Louisville Shops designed and built 282 new locomotives in four different wheel arrangements—2-8-0, 4-6-2, 0-8-0 and 2-8-2. The new power was produced under the direction of two skilled

Harold K. Vollrath Collection

Largest L&N ten-wheelers were eleven engines, Class G-13, built by Baldwin in 1903-4 for fast passenger service. Soon to be eclipsed by heavier Pacific types, the G-13 4-6-0s continued to perform well, some serving to the 1940s. Shown at Louisville in 1926, No. 316 was retired in 1948.

Baldwin constructed H-23 class 2-8-0 989 in 1903. These dependable freight hogs made up the bulk of L&N's freight fleet in the early years of the 20th century, with 200 H-23s joining the roster between 1903 and 1908. Baldwin, Rogers and South Louisville shared the orders.

motive power men, Millard F. Cox and Ernest O. Rollings. Cox was L&N's superintendent of machinery, while Rollings headed the South Louisville Shops. First designs were for a big 2-8-0 type for main line freight service, and between 1911-1914, the shops built 94 of these super Consols (classes H-28 and H-29). For mainline passenger service, two new 4-6-2 Pacific types were designed, classes K-3 and K-4, and from 1912 through 1920, over 60 of

these fine passenger engines were erected at South Louisville Yard and terminal chores were not forgotten by Cox and Rollings. A burly boilered eight-wheeler (0-8-0), class C-1, was designed, utilizing the 80-inch diameter boiler from the H-28s; and 34 of the big C's were constructed during the years 1915-23.

Cox and Rollings were masters of their trade. One of their innovations was the interchangability of parts forged or fabricated for

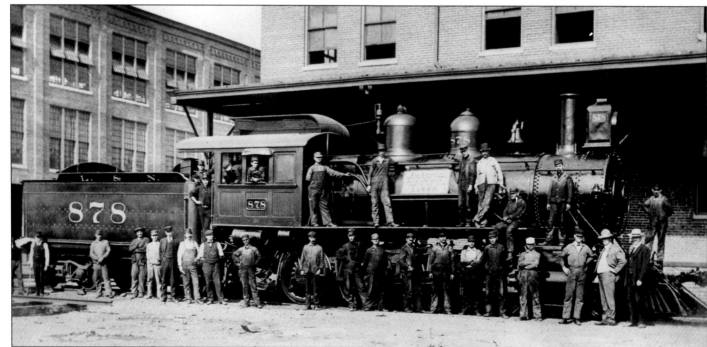

H-15 class no. 878 was the first locomotive repaired at the then-new South Louisville Shops. On June 1, 1905, a proud group of shopmen posed with the shiny 2-8-0.

the various types of locomotives. Such standardization of parts, not always practiced by other railroads back then, brought economies to L&N's motive power performance and maintenance and was another example of the fiscal conservatism and efficiency of the Old Reliable.

The largest and heaviest locomotives produced at South Louisville were the 96 J-1 and J-2 Class 2-8-2s, or Mikado types, turned out from 1914 through 1921.

When the J-1s appeared, not only were they the first of their wheel type on the L&N, but also they ranked among the most powerful 2-8-2s owned by any railroad then. Designed with huge fireboxes, mechanical stokers and low driving wheels, the big J's were quickly assigned to power heavy coal trains originating in the mine fields tapped by the Cumberland Valley and Eastern Kentucky Divisions.

Many L&N enginemen regarded the Js as the very best of the home-built steam power.

The South Louisville shops can claim credit for many things, and one of note was the assembly of a single locomotive, K-4 Pacific No. 238, in one week.

By 1918, World War I had made unprecedented traffic demands on U.S. railroads, and L&N President Milton H. Smith ordered a speed up on the delivery of a group of the new K-4s then a-building. On Monday, February 4, the 238 was scattered throughout the shop. Six days later, or by the weekend, steam coursed through 238's boiler and pipes,

and she soon after highballed away on her first trip. That record is still hailed industry-wide as an outstanding achievement of locomotive construction and craftsmanship. Because of higher labor and production costs, L&N's last new home-built locomotives were turned out in 1923. However, many of the well-designed South Louisville-built engines served on into the early 1950s, working right beside the new diesels.

Of course the L&N did not acquire all of its new power from its own erecting shops. Between 1900-1949, the American, Baldwin and Lima locomotive companies shared in building a number of engines. For example, from 1905 through 1943, American assembled some 450 locomotives for the L&N. These included 4-6-2, 4-8-2, 2-8-0, 2-8-2 and 0-8-0 types. More specifically, American (Schenectady, Brooks and Richmond shops) delivered over 200 2-8-2 Mikados in the 1500, 1700 and 1800 series, classes J-3 and J-4.

The United States Railroad Administration, which controlled the nation's railroads during and just after World War I, developed a series of basic locomotive designs for railroads, and in 1918-19, the agency assigned some 50 "standard" engines to the L&N, including six heavy 0-8-0s (Class C-2), five Pacifics (class K-5), 18 light Mikes (class J-3), and 20 heavy Mikes (class J-4).

The USRA power performed so well on the L&N that most all steam engines acquired by the company thereafter (or until the M-1s in 1942) followed basic USRA designs, albeit with

Harold K. Vollrath Collection

Some 60 old 2-8-0s were rebuilt as 0-6-0s by the L&N after 1900, many also receiving new boilers. B-6 class 623, originally turned out by Rogers as a 2-8-0 in 1886, rested between chores at Radnor Yard, Nashville, in 1940.

Harold K. Vollrath Collection

K-2A Pacific 152 is probably the most famous of all L&N steamers, if for no other reason than its longevity. At New Orleans in August 1933, the 4-6-2 waited her turn on a Gulf Coast commuter train. Donated to the Kentucky Railway Museum in 1957, No.152 was restored to operating condition in 1985 and at this writing still steams up and down former L&N Lebanon Branch trackage in Nelson County, Ky., now owned by KRM.

Harold K. Vollrath Collection

The H-25 and H-27 medium sized 2-8-0s, represented by 1181 pictured at Nashville in 1948, were an improved version of the successful H-23 class, and over 100 H-25/27s were built between 1907-1911 by Baldwin, Rogers and South Louisville. Some ran right up to dieselization in the early 1950s.

K-5 No. 266 was dolled up in dark green paint, pin stripes and lots of silver trim to handle the 1941 *Pan-American*. South Louisville enlarged the 266's tender to a 14,000-gallon capacity to reduce water stops and expedite the *Pan's* schedule, since a standard K-5 tender held just 10,000 gallons.

On April 22, 1949, Engineer U. G. Elrod and Fireman W. C. Greer and their L-1 416 had just arrived at Union Station, Louisville, with the last run of the seasonal *Florida Arrow*. After World War II, L-1's regularly handled the every-third day luxury train between Louisville and Montgomery. Auxiliary water car sported the train name.

L&N's first 2-8-2 Mikado types were designed and built at South Louisville, beginning in 1914. Intended for the coal fields, the big boilered J-1s and J-2s (the latter class an improved version) spent most of their years lugging Kentucky coal. No. 2400, first of the 62 J-1 and J-1As, was at DeCoursey in 1937.

Augmenting its home-built 0-8-0's, L&N ordered 26 USRA-designed heavy switchers, Class C-2, from Alco between 1919-25. No. 2154 rode the turntable at Evansville in the late 1940s.

refinements specified by Louisville.

Between 1920 and 1923, the L&N added 75 more J-3 Mikes to augment the initial USRA Lima engines of 1919. Of medium size and capacity, the J-3s were assigned to the more level divisions. Meanwhile, the first 20 heavy J-4s were joined by 145 similar engines, with the final 24 (class J-4A, from Baldwin in 1929) featuring Delta trailing trucks for the later addition of boosters. These big 2-8-2s became the principal main line freight locomotives, so

serving between Cincinnati-Birmingham and Cincinnati-Knoxville, and eventually running on to Atlanta and as far south as Mobile and Pensacola.

On the passenger side, the six big Pacifics of 1919 were joined by 20 more, Baldwin and American splitting the orders, in 1923-24. The K-5s became the favored engine for top assignments including the premiere *Pan-American* over much of the railroad in the 1920s and 30s. But to power long mainline limiteds and year-

Prior to advent of the M-1 class engines, heaviest L&N freight power were the 24 members of class J-4A. Essentially a booster-equipped J-4, the "Little 1900's" were concentrated on the toughest main line segments of the L&N. The 1906, at DeCoursey in 1937, prepared to return empty hoppers to Corbin.

To handle heavy 1920s passenger consists over hillier portions of the system, L&N in 1926 began acquiring 4-8-2 Mountain types based on the proven USRA design. The first of 22 class L-1 engines, no. 400 was on the Radnor ready tracks at Nashville in 1936. Old Reliable's passenger power featured the distinctive red/gold herald under cab windows, imitation gold lettering, silvered cylinder heads and running boards

round Florida trains by then moving over several divisions, L&N needed a yet bigger passenger engine, and in 1926, it purchased 16 4-8-2s (road class L-1) based on the USRA Light Mountain. Six more L-1s were ordered in 1930, both groups constructed by Baldwin. Ranging as far south as Mobile, the L-1s in fact spent more time on the hillier Cincy-Atlanta and Cincy-Birmingham mains. Displaced by E-units after 1942, the L-1s closed out their years in fast freight service.

Two groups of smallish secondhand Pacifics also joined the roster during the 1920s. Four K-6 Pacifics were acquired from the GM&N in 1921 (for Gulf Coast commuter runs, primarily), and seven K-8 light Pacifics came, with merger of the Louisville, Henderson & St. Louis in 1929. The latter engines saw service on passenger locals, mostly in Kentucky and in the coalfields.

Two "rare bird" engines need also to be mentioned. As noted before, L&N was not prone to experiment, but in the 1920s the road did sample two three-cylinder locomotives. An Alco-built USRA-designed heavy Mike, No. 1999, arrived in 1924. The next year, Alco sent down a heavy Pacific, No. 295. The pair did

not fare well in daily service, because of intensive maintenance required for their center cylinders. Both were sidelined during the Depression 1930s. But in 1940, a reprieve came for the Pacific, No. 295. At South Louisville, 295 was streamlined, losing her middle cylinder in the process, then went in service on the new *South Wind* streamliner that December. The 1999 was also rescued (although with third cylinder intact) and finished her career in hump duty at DeCoursey Yard. Incidentally, two other Pacifics, K-5s 275 and 277, were streamlined in 1940-41 for the *South Wind* and *Dixie Flagler* trains.

For switching chores, the L&N after 1900 utilized a batch of some 80 0-6-0s rebuilt by South Louisville and other shops from late nineteenth century 2-8-0s.

Baldwin and Alco supplied 35 new 0-6-0s between 1903-1907, and several more six-wheeled switchers were acquired secondhand in the 1920s. For heavy yard and transfer service, L&N relied on 60 0-8-0s, 34 as previously mentioned built by South Louisville in 1915-23, and 26 USRA design engines delivered between 1919 and 1925.

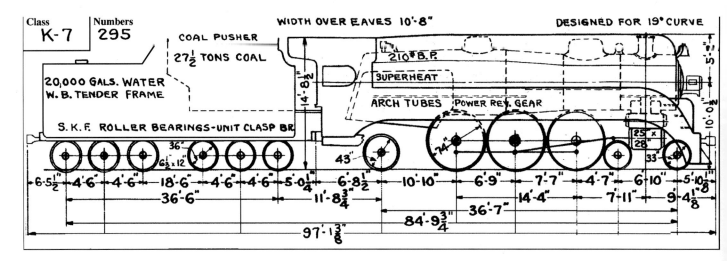

E.G. Baker Photo/L&N Historical Society

Bumped from *Wind* duties by diesels, the 295 was shown at Louisville in 1953 minus streamlining, finished her service life that year pulling local passenger trains on the Eastern Kentucky Division. See the diagram, above, for engine while streamlined

Harold K. Vollrath Collection

The 295's three-cylinder sister was heavy Mikado 1999. Initially used in coal train service, the engine was a machinists nightmare and spent her days in hump service at DeCoursey Yard where it was shown in 1946.

It's December 1940, and K-5 277 steams forth from South Louisville after being dressed up for the Chicago-Florida *Dixie Flagler*, which L&N moved between Evansville and Nashville. The big Pacific's color scheme is black, silver, with red and yellow trim.

Rescued from South Louisville's storage lines in fall 1940, Pacific 295 was streamlined and rebuilt with two 25"x28" cylinders and given a custom 20,000-gallon tender. New assignment for 295: speed the *South Wind* streamliner over the Louisville-Montgomery leg of its Chicago-Miami run.

Four M-1s came equipped with steam lines for World War II passenger service. A Decade later, the quartet had one final fling at varnish for the 1956 Kentucky Derby, powering Cincinnati-Louisville specials that year. Late Derby afternoon, 1963 and 1961 shared the 10th Street engine tracks at Louisville with FP7 612 before returning their specials to Cincy.

Big Emma

The era of American superpower steam power was represented on the L&N by its great M-1 2-8-4 locomotives; the first 20 came from Baldwin in 1942 and 1944. Their success prompted purchase of 22 additional engines built by Lima in 1949 to handle the upsurge in Eastern Kentucky coal business. The Lima M-1s were L&N's last new steam locomotives and were also among the last commercially built steam in the U.S.

Incredible machines, the M-1s sadly were short-lived but continued to lug coal on the Cincinnati, Eastern Kentucky, and Cumberland Valley divisions right up to complete dieselization in late 1956. Operating crews on the "KY" between Corbin and Cincinnati gave the modern 2-8-4s the nickname that endured to this day: "Big Emmas!"

Delivered in summer and fall 1942, the first M-1s could not have come at a more opportune time. Initially assigned to the Cincinnati Division and to DeCoursey - Corbin runs, they gave real meaning to the term "fast freight" in

L&N's employee timetables. Wartime tonnage ratings had to be revised upwards because the M-1 provided even more power at the drawbar than was predicted by Baldwin's specs. Four Big Emmas from the first order were equipped with steam and signal lines to handle heavy passenger consists, including the *Southland* and *Flamingo,* on the same Cincy-Corbin route. With roller bearings on all axles, 69" drivers, 25"x32" cylinders and 65,290 pounds of tractive effort (supplemented by 14,100 pounds from trailing truck boosters), the 2-8-4s turned in stellar performances on coal drags, manifest freights, passenger trains AND troop specials. Big Emmas were perfectly matched for what L&N called on them to do.

To meet post-World War II coal traffic demands, L&N in 1946 began modernizing its operations in the Eastern Kentucky coalfields. Still firmly committed to the steam standard for freight, the road ordered 22 more M-1s from Lima to handle the increased coalfields traffic. Operationally, the Emmas worked the entire length of the Eastern Kentucky Division from Neon to Patio (Winchester) and beyond to

Frank E. Ardrey/L&N Collection/University of Louisville Archives

Diesels eventually bumped the L-1 4-8-2s from choice assignments on main line "varnish," and the engines finished their careers in freight service. Passing NC&StL's Hills Park Yard in Atlanta, the 417 headed north with a K&A Division fast freight on May 19, 1951.

L&N Collection/University of Louisville Archives

USRA also sent its "Heavy Mikado" to the L&N. Pleased with the first 20 engines (Class J-4), delivered from Brooks in 1918, the road in the 1920s added 121 more J-4s, the class becoming its standard main line heavy freight locomotive. At South Louisville just after receiving class repairs in 1948, 1770 also displayed L&N's standard steam freight "livery."

L&N Collection/University of Louisville Archives

No. 1954 represented steam's high water mark on the L&N. Baldwin delivered 1954 as part of the initial 14-engine 1942 order for the M-1s L&N never called them "Berkshires," ordering six more in 1944. Lima got the 1948 order for the final 22 "Big Emmas."

Joe G. Collias Photo

Extra 1974 North, a Corbin-DeCoursey "Main Tracker" off the CV, prepared to drop the second helping M-1 at Patio Tower, Winchester, Ky., in August 1950. The 1974 next pulled ahead to clear the second Emma. A third Emma, which coupled on behind the caboose at the bottom of Winchester Hill at Ford, then helped start the 136-car tonnage train before cutting off "on the fly" just past the tower.

Baldwin-built M-1 1956 accelerated a southward EK empty hopper train from DeCoursey Yard about 1944. Shot shows to good advantage the huge 25-ton, 20,000-gallon capacity M-l tender. Built for coal service, "Big Emmas" as crews called them were also adept at rolling fast freight or passengers. Diagram, below, gives specifications for engines.

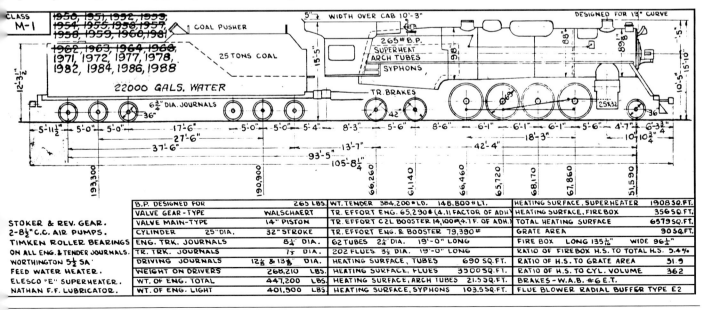

STOKER & REV. GEAR.
2-8½"C.C. AIR PUMPS.
TIMKEN ROLLER BEARINGS
ON ALL ENG. & TENDER JOURNALS.
WORTHINGTON 5½ SA
FEED WATER HEATER.
ELESCO "E" SUPERHEATER.
NATHAN F.F. LUBRICATOR.

B.P. DESIGNED FOR		265 LBS.	WT. TENDER 384,200 # LD. 148,800 # LT.		HEATING SURFACE, SUPERHEATER		1908 SQ. FT.
VALVE GEAR - TYPE		WALSCHAERT	TR. EFFORT ENG. 65,290 # (4.11 FACTOR OF ADH)		HEATING SURFACE, FIREBOX		356 SQ. FT.
VALVE MAIN - TYPE		14" PISTON	TR. EFFORT C2L BOOSTER 14,100 # (4.71 F. OF ADH)		TOTAL HEATING SURFACE		6579 SQ. FT.
CYLINDER 25" DIA.		32" STROKE	TR. EFFORT ENG. & BOOSTER 79,390 #		GRATE AREA		90 SQ. FT.
ENG. TRK. JOURNALS	8¼" DIA.		62 TUBES 2¼" DIA. 19'-0" LONG		FIRE BOX LONG 135½" WIDE 96¼"		
TR. TRK. JOURNALS	7¼" DIA.		202 FLUES 3½" DIA. 19'-0" LONG		RATIO OF FIREBOX H.S. TO TOTAL H.S.	5.4%	
DRIVING JOURNALS	12⅝ & 13⅝" DIA.		HEATING SURFACE, TUBES	690 SQ. FT.	RATIO OF H.S. TO GRATE AREA	51.9	
WEIGHT ON DRIVERS	268,210 LBS.		HEATING SURFACE, FLUES	3500 SQ. FT.	RATIO OF H.S. TO CYL. VOLUME	362	
WT. OF ENG. TOTAL	447,200 LBS.		HEATING SURFACE, ARCH TUBES	21.5 SQ. FT.	BRAKES - W.A.B. # 6 E.T.		
WT. OF ENG. LIGHT	401,500 LBS.		HEATING SURFACE, SYPHONS	103.5 SQ. FT.	FLUE BLOWER RADIAL BUFFER TYPE E2		

The busy Flomaton, Ala., junction boasted one of L&N's newer coaling stations, which was built in 1943, late in the steam era. The impressive structure still stood, as of 1995. L&N's Gulf Coast-tFlorida line (PD/P&A Subdivisions) via Pensacola left the main line at Flomaton.

DeCoursey on coal trains. At Elkatawa Hill just west of Jackson, northward trains encountered a 4.5 mile-long, 1.0 per cent grade. To open up the bottleneck grade, L&N, in an unusual move, bought five EMD F3 diesels in 1948. M-1s of course brought trains over from Neon and Hazard, but at Elkatawa, three of the new F3s coupled on behind the caboose to help trains uphill. Once over the grade, the M-1s took trains on to Ravenna and DeCoursey.

In conjunction with the F3 diesel helpers at Elkatawa, it was possible not only to replace two steam helper engines but also to increase the tonnage ratings of Cincinati-bound EK coal trains from 6650 to 9500 tons. The investment in new steam and diesel power, as well as the installation of CTC and other track improvements, helped the L&N to save $1-million annually on its important Eastern Kentucky coal-hauling trunk.

On the Cumberland Valley Division to the south, the M-1s initially worked Corbin to Loyall "turns" but later became preferred power for coal trains off the Poor Fork Branch from Chad to Corbin and on the double-daily Corbin-Norton, Va., fast freights. In time

Doubleheaded J-4's worked hard through suburban St. Matthews, Ky., in 1945 with a DeCoursey-Louisville fast freight. The tough Short Line often required two big Mikes on through freight trains.

Emmas worked up and down the Short Line between Cincy and the big shop at South Louisville for class repairs; they wheeled fast freights and Kentucky Derby Specials with equal aplomb on that route and also were authorized to run on the Lebanon Branch and the EK Division's "Old Road" from Winchester to Anchorage via Lexington.

In service, the M-1s boasted high availability and low maintenance and were able to show a 12 percent increase in fuel savings over the next best steam class, the J-4. L&N's management, obviously pleased with the performance of the M-1s, declared that the engines were one of the principal factors enabling the road to increase train-mile per train-hour from 14.9 in 1942 to 16.5 in May, 1949; that increase in speed occurred simultaneously with tonnage-per-train increases, L&N added. The zenith of steam on the Old Reliable, Big Emmas were truly engines for all seasons.

The Diesel Era

Remarkably enough, hints of motive power other than steam appeared on Old Reliable as early as 1900. Sometime during that first decade, a self-propelled gas car made trial runs on the NF&S (Nashville, Florence & Sheffield) subdivision.

Little was known (or later reported) about the runs or the diminutive four-wheeled gas car. But, in 1928, L&Ners did witness a more permanent reminder of things to come, with the purchase of Brill gas-electric car No. 3600. Intended to replace steam passenger trains on branch and secondary routes, the 3600 was tried out on several runs, then settled in on, again, the NF&S to hold down a Columbia, Tenn.-Florence, Ala., schedule for some years.

Out of service by the mid 1950s, the car was later retired.

But, back to the late 1930s. L&N's management was coming under increased pressure from Louisville city fathers and others elsewhere to reduce smoke emissions from its locomotives. To placate those concerns, the road purchased two diesel-electric switchers for the Louisville Terminals. Alco H660 No. 10 arrived in September 1939, soon followed by Electro-Motive SW1 No. 11. The two engines performed well and by 1941, twelve more switchers (supplied by Alco, Baldwin and EMD) had joined the duo. Eventually, L&N's yard switcher fleet included Alco S1s, S2s and S3s, Baldwin VO660s and VO1000s, and EMD NW2s, SW7s, SW9s and SW1200s. GE contributed two 70-tonners, nos.. 125 and 126

L&N Collection/University of Louisville Archive.

L&N's original road freight units were five F3's, bought from EMD in 1948. Nicknamed "Black Cats," the units came in "plain black" to lesser agitation of the Eastern Kentucky mining industry. Soon after delivery, the units prepared to push a coal train up the EK's Elkatawa Hill at Gentry the service for which they were purchased.

Both: L&N Collection/University of Louisville Archives

L&N's first diesel-electric was Alco HH660 No. 10. The somber black locomotive, its lettering in imitation gold, was on the South Louisville Shops transfer table shortly after delivery in September 1939. Also in fall 1939, Electro-Motive Corporation (then called EMC) sent down SW1 No. 11, amid a sea of steam power at South Louisville, the LaGrange product showed L&N'ers just what was beneath its glossy black hood.

(later becoming nos.. 98 and 99) for light rail use around Nashville.

In June 1941 the L&N announced it was in the market for 18 to 22 steam passenger locomotives. A medium-size 4-8-4 (similar to RF&P engines then in service) was considered. Electro-Motive proposed paired E6 passenger diesels instead, pointing out that L&N's miles of wooden trestles along the Gulf Coast could not handle big steam; the diesels, their weight spread across 12 axles, could run all the way from Cincinnati to New Orleans. L&N also received a proposal from Alco (for similar DL109/DL110 A-B pairs), but opted for 16 E6s, which were delivered in spring and summer, l942 (EMD also supplied E7s in 1945 for the new *Humming Bird* and *Georgian* streamliners, and again in 1949).

The 16 wartime EMD E6s showed L&N what road diesels could do, highballing war-swollen *Azaleans* and *Pan-Americans* from the Ohio Valley straight through to the Gulf Coast, then turning within hours to head north. The high utilization of the passenger units—and later with road freight diesels—contrasted sharply with performance from L&N's aging steam fleet, many engines of World War I vintage or older. As management weighed merits of diesel versus steam, more data flowed in from experience with the EK Division F3 EMD helper units as well as from neighboring Clinchfield and NC&StL, both already em-barked on dieselization programs by the late 1940s.

During 1948, three F3s (which EK crews had dubbed "Black Cats") were matched against M-1 1965 for dynamometer car-monitored runs on the Cincy-Louisville Short Line. The tests revealed significant operating savings over steam. Later that fall and again in 1949, two of the new "Cats" barnstormed over other divisions of the system. Some inevitable conclusions came to light: the availability and high utilization of the diesels, coupled with economies from fewer, longer trains moving at higher speeds, reduced fuel consumption and lower maintenance costs, strongly justified dieselization to L&N's cost-conscious management. In short, it was time for steam to go.

In 1950, the year of L&N's centennial, large orders were placed with Alco and EMD for diesels of all types. The new power included EMD F7s, GP7s, E8s, Alco FA and FB-2s, RS-3s, and other units. By November 1952, the locomotive fleet was split, with 412 diesels in service as against 345 steam engines, many already stored pending retirement and by year's end, four operating divisions were completely dieselized. There was a notable exception—the coal fields in eastern Kentucky. That was still "Big Emma" territory! But, by 1954, even the Cincinnati Division's "KY" main, the EK, and CV were seeing diesels. Black and cream Geeps and Alcos began infiltrating the very heart of coal country, where L&N steam locomotives burned what they hauled.

For all practical purposes, regular service steam came to a close on November 3, 1956, when M-1 No. 1950 brought a coal train into DeCoursey from Ravenna. But over on the subsidiary Carrollton Railroad (also in Northern Kentucky), "lend-lease" J-4 Mike No. 1882 labored on. By late January 1957, L&N found a spare diesel for the Carrollton. On a cold, rainy January 28th, EMD switcher No. 2294 brought a Short Line local freight up from Louisville to Worthville, Ky., L&N's junction with the short line, where the veteran Mike was standing by to make the exchange. With a custom whistle that once graced K-5 Pacific No. 278, the 1882 made one more glorious romp up main line trackage to DeCoursey. When her fire was dropped that evening, steam was indeed finished on the Old Reliable. All remaining steam locomotives (M-1s or J-4s) were soon after retired and officially stricken from the roster.

Citing accomplishments from dieselizing freight services (which began in 1950), President John Tilford on the eve of full dieselization wrote his board of directors and company stock holders: "Although net ton miles increased 16 per cent, train miles decreased 17 per cent. Locomotive miles dropped 19 per cent, and train hours decreased to 21 per cent. In the same period, gross ton miles per train hour increased over 45 per cent." Millions, concluded Mr. Tilford, were saved by the switch from steam to diesel.

In August 1957, after the NC&StL merger, L&N's total diesel fleet stood at 734 units, which included 138 "new" diesels acquired from the smaller road.

Power was classified as follows: 112 cab or "A" units, for passenger and/or freight service; 15 booster or "B" units, also dual-service; 158 cab or "A" and booster "B" units, freight only; 42 dual service "GP" or road switcher units; 195 freight "GP" road switchers and 211 yard switchers

The Second Generation

With the exception of five GP18s, delivered in April 1960, the L&N handled all yard, freight and passenger traffic without new additions for the five year period following the end of steam. Faced, however, with the challenge to speed up freight schedules, lower operating costs and replace the older units in the fleet, the road ordered its first "second generation" diesel power in 1962. Arriving that summer from EMD were 29 GP30s (2,250 horsepower, each). The new power continued the "low-nose" look introduced on the L&N by the five GP18s delivered two years before. But unlike that somber black group, the new GP30s were the first new power to display a new L&N color scheme, Confederate gray and yellow. The new colors closely matched the paint scheme applied earlier to GP18 no. 460.

Success of the initial GP30s sent L&N back to LaGrange in 1963 for another 29 units, and

Dick Sharpless/Frank Ardrey Collection
An Alco FA-2-powered freight swung through a curve on the K&A Division's "Hook and Eye" subdivision just south of Canton, Ga., in June 1954. No. 364's fireman gave an enthusiastic wave to the photographer.

Between 1951-54, Alco also built over 70 RS-3 road switchers for the L&N. RS-3's were normally assigned to the CV, EK and K&A Divisions, as well as to the Lebanon Branch. The exhaust stack mounted lengthwise and the lack of M.U. cables were clues that the 173, shown at Corbin, was photographed not long after delivery. All RS-3s were later modified.

upstart General Electric also delivered 13 U-25Bs (2,500 h.p.). From the used motive power market, the road picked up some bargain-basement ex-Rutland and Lehigh & New England Alco cab units, road switchers and yard units in 1963. Receiving "quickie" repaint jobs, the units went right into service.

Few stayed around for more than a year or so; their value was greater as trade-ins for more new power.

The year 1964 was a memorable one for L&N motive power. That year, EMD delivered 16 GP35s, GE added another 14 U25-Bs, and Alco kicked in with six C-420s. The big event, however, was delivery of 12 six-motor Alco C-628s, the first so-called "big power" for the L&N. A year later, the trend toward "six-axles" (as L&Ners labeled them) was in full swing, with 22 SD35s and four SDP35s coming from EMD, four more C-628s from Alco, and GE sending down 18 U25-Cs.

The road also picked up three used E7s and four E8s from the Frisco to augment its own geriatric E-unit fleet.

To maximize utilization of its motive power fleet, the L&N in the early 1960s set up a Locomotive Utilization Bureau (LUB) at Louisville. With continual reports from the operating divisions, LUB staff closely monitored all engine assignments and train movements, also directing power where needed; units due inspections and scheduled maintenance were flagged, as were those out of service.

Eventually, the LUB merged with a System Train Operations Office, also in Louisville, and in 1976, the combined office and its staff were enlarged and transformed into the Transportation Control Center, complete with computers, improved communications and wall-length displays of operations system-wide.

Delivery, meanwhile, of new SD40s, Alco C-630s and C-420s and GE four- and six-axles (U-28Cs U-28Bs, U-30Bs and U-30Cs) rounded out L&N's motive power acquisitions in the late 1960s. The 420s, incidentally, were the last new Alcos delivered to the L&N before the firm closed its doors in 1969. Several former C&EI and Tennessee Central units were also picked up, as portions of those railroads were merged into the larger system. Eight used Oro Dam U-25Cs also found their way into the roster in 1967. From 1962 through 1972, the L&N purchased over 500 second generation units, adding 1,083,850 more horsepower to its fleet

New EMD GP38s and GP38-2s began arriving during the early 1970s to supplement existing road power. L&N sought to balance its four- and six-axle power. The more powerful "sixes" were used on coal trains and on the hillier divisions, while the four axle units worked on the more level lines. To upgrade yard service, new EMD SW1500s were bought from 1970 to 1972. At the same time some former Alco switchers and RS3s were also converted to yard slugs then.

L&N Collection/University of Louisville Archives

L&N went back to EMD in 1951 for four E8s, and the 794 and 796 were spotted at South Louisville for the company photographer soon after their arrival that summer.

Later in the decade, EMD and GE delivered more road and yard power (GP38-2s and 40-2s, SD40-2s, MP15ACs, SD38-2s for the Boyles Hump, B23-7s, and C30-7s). The company also tested EMD GP50s and SD50s, and in early 1983, the first SD50s went into eastern Kentucky coal service (former L&N divisions of the new Seaboard System). The 25 SD50s were actually ordered by the L&N in 1982, but were delivered in the new paint scheme of the Seaboard System.

As noted in the previous chapter on coal traffic, the 1970s witnessed severe motive power shortages on the L&N. The road simply did not have enough power to move the great increases in business, particularly coal. Under ICC order, corporate parent Seaboard Coast Line sent up 100 units to help handle the onslaught of traffic. Some of SCL's older Alco and EMD units were later transferred to L&N ownership and integrated into its roster. Power was also leased from other railroads until L&N could purchase its own new units.

Steve Patterson

Mated with an ex-RS-3 slug, Alco C420 1303 took a break from working the north end of the West Yard at Corbin in August 1980. L&N's own purchase of C420s in the mid 1960s was modest, but the TC and Monon mergers brought another batch of the type to the larger road. Then, with the Family Lines formation in the early 1970s, yet another group from SCL came north to L&N country to swell the C420 series to over 70 units.

189

L&N Collection/University of Louisville Archives

In the late 1950s, L&N began equipping its road diesels with two-way radio. The engineer of F7A 802 demonstrated the new feature at South Louisville. It was then that the road also began repainting all power in an austere black or blue color scheme, with gold block lettering and simplified heralds.

Mid-trains and Helpers

During the mid-1960s, L&N conducted experiments with mid-train "slave" units on coal trains. The mid-train power was controlled by the engineer in the lead unit. Two variations were tried: Veteran F7A no. 830 was fitted with a strain gauge and other instrumentation so that it could respond to stress placed on the front drawbar (coupler). The technique allowed the 830 and other mid-train coupled units to work as helper units totally independent of the engineer's control. As the slack ran out in the train, the 830 would "load up" until the tension on its drawbar was reduced. The experiment lasted less than a year.

The "RMU" or Remote Multiple Unit system, a somewhat more successful mid-train power technique, was next tried. The system, similar to "RMU" used on the Southern Railway and other lines, utilized radio-equipped power controlled from a lead locomotive. L&N outfitted several SDP35s as "masters" or control units and or retired Alco and EMD B-units as mid-train radio-receiver cars. The RMU application on Old Reliable was intended to move huge coal trains from Corbin and the EK Sub to DeCoursey. Alas, in actual practice, the mammoth trains rarely got over the division without numerous stops for broken knuckles, pulled drawheads and other problems. The L&N soon reverted to more conventional operations in its eastern Kentucky coalfields.

Even after the end of steam, the L&N continued to maintain helper districts on several of its significant grades. One was at the previously described Elkatawa Hill on the Eastern Kentucky Division between Jackson and Ravenna.

Another was the former NC&StL's Cumberland Mountain pusher district, based at Cowan, Tenn., on the Nashville-Atlanta main line. Occasionally, diesel helper power was used at Muldraugh Hill, south of Louisville. With the shift of coal traffic southward in the 1970s, L&N re-established helper service in 1978 over Duff Mountain, from Chaska to Duff, Tenn., on the Corbin-Atlanta main line. There, the two assigned six-axle units pushed heavy southbound coal trains over that bottleneck ruling grade.

Motive Power Paint Schemes

L&N steam locomotives were painted the same shade of color as the ink in the company's books: basic black. Lettering was imitation gold. Several roundhouses and shops—notably Corbin, Evansville

Wm. C. Tayse/L&N Collection, University of Louisville Archives
During the 1960s, L&N tested several mid-train remote control systems for motive power on long coal trains in Eastern Kentucky. One such system, applied to F7 830, utilized sensors in the unit's coupler to gauge power requirements. In September 1964, the 830, paired with RS3s 132 and 239, ground up the long grade from Ravenna to Winchester, Ky., with Midwest-destined coal.

and Paris, Tenn., embellished their assigned passenger engines with silver-trimmed tires, running boards and cylinder head covers. Still, the system standard for steam power was solid black with little or no trim. Exceptions were the 42 M-1s, which came with stripped driving wheel tires and yellow running boards, the only freight power to be so decorated. From the 1930s on, passenger engines featured the familiar red and gold L&N herald mounted just under the cab window. Also perpetuated by Old Reliable was the old custom of painting the locomotive number on the front headlight lens. The practice aided in identifying at night approaching trains and their locomotives at meets in train-order territory. Until the mid-'50s, some F- and E-units were so numbered.

Big Pacifics 275, 277 and 295 received special treatment for their *Dixie Flagler* and *South Wind* streamliner assignments. Side panels were silver edged in red or yellow trim, while boilers, dome casings, wheels and trucks were black.

A post-World War II shopping transformed the 295 into a tuscan red engine to match the PRR-owned *South Wind* equipment. At least one other K-5, the 266, was painted dark green with gold trim in 1941 for service on the *Pan-American*. Several other K-5 Pacifics received double stripes along their tenders as did the M-1 2-8-4s.

Color schemes for L&N diesel power varied over the years. The first two yard engines—Nos.. 10 and 11—were painted steam engine black with yellow lettering. The E6 passenger units of 1942 introduced the beautiful blue and cream colors with orange trim, red and gold nose heralds and gold script lettering, which with variations lasted until 1958. The 1948 EK Division F3 freighters arrived in solid black to avoid invoking the wrath of coal industry folk in Eastern Kentucky. During the 1950s, newly purchased freight diesels were painted very similarly to the passenger units, except that black was substituted for dark blue. Then in 1958, L&N followed a national trend to simplify locomotive liveries and adopted an all-black (freight) and all-blue (passenger) scheme, each with gold block lettering and circular nose-mounted heralds (for cab units).

Ron Flanary

On August 4, 1965, a pair of E6s at Union Station, Louisville, suggested the transition under way in color schemes. At left, in the late 1950s "basic blue," the 751 with a trailing E8 took water while pausing with the southbound *Pan-American*. At right, "protection power" stood by, lead unit 756 recently modified with a functional sealed beam headlight and repainted in the newer, more attractive gray-yellow scheme.

J. Parker Lamb

In September 1959, two years after the L&N-NC&StL merger, ex-NC power could still be found at the important Bruceton, Tenn., division point. Black paint covered former NC "blue and gray" for cab units or "red and gold" for most road switchers. In renumbering, L&N merely added "1000" to the original numbers of the NC&StL road units.

In 1962, GP18 No. 460 introduced the familiar gray and yellow color scheme, which was also applied to the new GP30s that arrived later in the year. With some variations, the gray-yellow scheme was used until 1977, when a new "Family Lines" French gray scheme was adopted by all member roads. Ownership for each member road was indicated by the initials "L&N" (or "CRR", "SCL", etc.) under cab windows.

The Final Engines

L&N motive power history came to a close on January 1, 1983, as the road and other members of the "Family" were merged into the newly created Seaboard System Railroad. Although 25 new SD50s were then on order, the big six-axles were delivered two months later in Seaboard System gray paint.

From the diminutive wood-burning eight-

J. Parker Lamb

South Louisville designers tinkered with several experimental paint schemes during the late 1950s. This particular variation, displayed by F7A 913, featured a gray body with red lettering and triple diamond herald. The unique unit was photographed at Attalla, Ala., in December 1957.

L&N Collection/University of Louisville Archives

The first low-nose unit on the railroad was GP18 460, one of five "rebuilds" from older F7s and GPs done by EMD in 1960. Although delivered in black, the 460 was selected to test the new gray and yellow paint scheme and was pictured at Louisville in April 1962 with freshly painted box cars for a promotional film.

J. Parker Lamb

In service just long enough to pick up a thin coat of road grime, GP30 1005 led three sisters on a southbound fast freight up Seven Mile Hill into Tullahoma, Tenn., in August 1963. Former NC&StL mainline trackage was first to get the new second generation power, which replaced travel-weary F3s and F7s.

J. Parker Lamb

On the doubletracked Birmingham Division mainline at Brentwood, Tenn. just south of Nashville, ancient American steam shovel No. 39 did some ditching work, with GE 70-tonner no. 98 powering the train. The GE, later re-engined with an Alco 251B, and a mate worked around the Nashville Terminals as well as on several regional branch lines before being sold to private industry.

wheelers of the Civil War years to steam's apex in the form of the massive M-1 "Big Emmas," and from lowly yard diesels of 1939-40 to the high horsepower six-axles of the 1970s and early 80s. That was L&N's motive power story, long and colorful!

L&N's first road diesels were 16 paired E6's delivered by Electro-Motive in spring and summer of 1942. Initially numbered in the 450-series, with A and B suffixes to denote the two units in each set, the engines were later renumbered into the 750- and 770- blocks. Their first summer on the property, the 450, 456 and 454 with mates were serviced outside at South Louisville.

It was in the mid 1960s that L&N also began buying six-axle power for the coal fields and for hillier mainline routes, and all three builders Alco, EMD and GE supplied the road with big hood units. In April 1974, examples from the three firms lined up at the DeCoursey engine terminal. From left to right were Alco C630 1425, EMD SDP35 1222, and GE U30C 1545.

Dixie Line Motive Power— The NC&StL

Basically a north-south bridge route, the NC&StL for much of its century-plus history was to follow somewhat different motive power practices than its neighbor and (after 1880) parent, L&N. The road's principal antecedents, the Nashville & Chattanooga and Nashville & Northwestern, relied almost exclusively on 4-4-0 American types to power their trains. Eight-wheelers continued to dominate the NC&StL roster after the 1873 reorganization, although several 4-6-0s and 2-8-0s worked as Cumberland Mountain pushers during the post-Civil War decades. But, beginning in 1880, the NC&StL began buying low-drivered 4-6-0 Ten-wheelers for main line freight service, a group of 15, class G1, coming from the Rogers Works between '80-83. Over the next two decades, more than 50 of the type, all produced by Rogers and in class G-2, were added to the roster.

When the Western & Atlantic (owned by the State of Georgia) was leased to the NC&StL in 1890, mostly 4-4-0s, a few 4-6-0s and a handful of switchers came with the deal. Two W&A engines, the *General* and *Texas,* had gained notoriety from the Civil War "Great Locomotive Chase" episode (or Andrews Raid) in April 1862. Saved from the scrap line, the "General" reposed in honorable retirement for decades on the concourse of the Chattanooga Union Station. Then, in 1961, the old war engine was sent to the South Louisville Shops to be overhauled for Civil War commemorative events beginning in 1962. Much earlier, the *Texas* was displayed in the basement of Atlanta's Cyclorama.

After 1899, 2-8-0s and 2-8-2s were selected by the NC&StL for mainline freight service. The Baldwin-built H-5-class, 24 delivered that year, marked the first significant use of Consolidation-type engines on the road. Baldwin later delivered 51 heavier 2-8-0s, in classes H-6, H-7 and H-8. The Mikado type appeared in 1915 with delivery (by Baldwin) of the first of 29 2-8-2s, road class L-1, which were eventually to run over the entire system. N&C crews nicknamed the versatile Mikes "Jitneys." Then in 1918, the USRA assigned 10 light Mikes (from Alco). In common with L&N's practice, the road ordered 12 copies (class L-2) from Baldwin in 1922- 1923. The Eddystone-built engines came "souped up," with cast trailing trucks, boosters and Vanderbilt tenders.

One of the L-1 Mikes, the 616, was the subject of experiments during 1918, as the NC&StL attempted to wring more tractive effort from its engines. West Nashville Shops

Harold K. Vollrath Collection

From Rogers in 1889, No. 40 was typical of NC&StL's fleet of eight-wheelers. Relegated to branch line work after World War I, the old D-5 class engine was at Bruceton, Tenn., in 1935, two years before being scrapped.

H. C. Hill/L&N Collection, U of L Archives

Baldwin-built K-1A Pacific 508 was ready to go back to work in May 1930 after an overhaul at the West Nashville Shops. The "Dixie Line" herald was prominent on the 4-6-2's Vanderbilt tender.

slipped cylinders, wheels and running gear from an older 2-8-0 beneath the tender of the 616 to create a 2-8-2/2-8-0 Duplex. NC&StL found (as did the Southern about the same time with a 2-10-2 duplex) that the Mike couldn't supply enough steam for two sets of cylinders; and too, the ever diminishing weight of coal and water in the tender reduced the "tractor" engine's pulling power. The tests were soon nixed, and the 616 reverted back to her original wheel arrangement.

Five Russian Decapods were also acquired during World War I, spending most of their later years on branch lines and in yards. For Cumberland Mountain Pusher duties, three massive compound 2-8-8-2s, road class M-1, were purchased in 1915. Too heavy to run elsewhere on the line, the plodding Mallets worked up and down Cumberland's grades until after World War II, when they were replaced by pairs of Mikes.

In the 1890s, Ten-wheelers began to take over NC&StL's main line passenger trains. Several were bought new from Rogers, and five of the 1880s low drivered freight Ten-wheelers were rebuilt for varnish assignments. Then, between 1902-1908, Baldwin and Rogers supplied 16 engines in classes G-6, G-7 and G-8. The seven G-8s, built as four-cylinder balanced compounds, were later rebuilt by the West Nashville shops as conventional two-cylinder engines. Baldwin delivered another four Ten-Wheelers in 1909, but in service, the engines performed poorly and were recycled by Eddystone in 1912 as the NC&StL's first 4-6-2s (which became class K-1). That year, Baldwin also supplied eight heavier Pacifics, class K-2. Two were later streamlined (in 1940 and 1947) for the *Dixie Flager* and *City of Memphis* trains. Final 4-6-2s were eight light class K-1A engines, built in 1915 by Baldwin for Atlanta Division service.

L&N Collection,
University of Louisville Archives

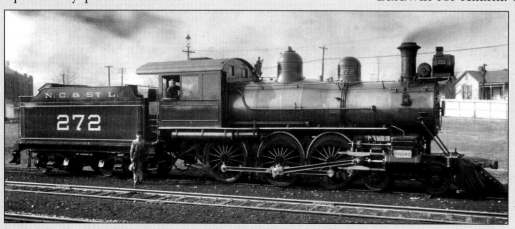

At West Nashville Shops when new, NC&StL 272 was a class G-7 4-6-0 built by Rogers in 1904 these were last engines delivered to the road by that builder. Some of the G-class ten-wheelers (several also multi-cylindered) were later rebuilt with piston valves, superheaters and Walschaert valve gear.

Eight-drivered dual service power showed up in 1919 in the guise of five USRA light Mountains, class J1, from Alco. The 4-8-2s were followed in 1922 and 1925 by eight similar engines by Baldwin. As with the second group of L-2s Mikes, the newer 4-8-2s sported Delta trailing trucks, boosters, and feedwater heaters. During the 1920s, one of the J's, the 550, was painted a dark maroon to pull NC&StL's flagship limited, the *Dixie Flyer*.

Over the years, NC normally assigned its older 2-8-0s for yard and transfer service. However, between 1891-1904 the road did purchase 17 0-6-0s for light switching duty from Rogers and Baldwin. In the teens and early 20s, it also converted seven 2-8-0s to 0-8-0s by removing their lead trucks.

five engines, road class J-2, incorporated such features as one-piece cast frames, feedwater heaters, large fireboxes and higher capacity boilers. Officially, the new 4-8-4s became "Dixies." However, a special design feature was to provide a more enduring nickname. Lateral-motion driving wheel boxes on the first and second axles enabled J-2s to literally "glide" in and out of the NC's numerous curves. To the men who ran and fired them, the J-2s became "Gliders!"

World War II poured unprecedented traffic across the NC&StL system, and badly needing more motive power, Superintendent Darden got an OK to duplicate the fine J-2 design with 20 more 4-8-4s, which were delivered in two groups of ten from Alco in 1942-3. Classed as

Second batch of World War II "Dixies," Nos.. 580-589 were assembled in 1943 by Alco's Schenectady works. Material shortages prevented application of decorative side skirts applied to the 1942 "Yellow Jacket" J3s, and so NC engine crews dubbed the 1943 engines "Stripes!"

Gliders, Yellow Jackets and Stripes

Perhaps the best known chapter in Dixie Line's modern steam story was written by its 25 remarkable 4-8-4s, which handled the lion's share of mainline traffic from 1930 on, or until dieselization after World War II. The story began in 1929 when Clarence M. Darden, the NC's capable motive power chief, headed a design team to produce a new dual-service 4-8-4. Delivered in 1930 by Alco, the

J-3s, The new Dixies came with semi-Vanderbilt tenders on six-wheel trucks, cast steel frames and cylinder saddles, Timken roller bearings throughout plus semi-streamlined nose cones. The 1942 engines were embellished with yellow side skirts, a feature the '43 engines lacked, due to war-time material restrictions. Crews dubbed the first ten engines "Yellow Jackets," while the second ten, with their single yellow-edged running boards and tender stripes, became "Stripes."

NC&StL installed new 100-foot long turntables at Atlanta, Bruceton, Chattanooga and Nashville to accommodate the new 4-8-4s.

Whether Glider, Yellow Jacket, or Stripe, the J-2 and J-3 class Dixies contributed mightily to NC&StL's achievement during World War II in transporting huge volumes of military and civilian passenger traffic as well as record freight tonnages. In common with all other NC steam power, the medium-weight 4-8-4s featured flanged or "capped" stacks. NC&StL steam expired in early January 1953 when H7 2-8-0 No. 406 rolled the Union City Branch local into Bruceton, Tenn., for the last time.

Dieselization

Excepting its 25 modern 4-8-4s, NC&StL's steam locomotive fleet after World War II was a geriatric lot. By 1947, over half were over 30 years old. But by that date, diesels were no longer strangers to the Dixie Line, what with a group of switchers already at work in stations and yards and EMD E7s breezing between Nashville and Atlanta with the new *Georgian* streamliners. Alco S1s and a single EMD SW1 had been purchased in 1941, in the wake of L&N's trend to dieselize certain terminals. As the decade progressed, more Alco S1s and S2s, five EMD NW2s and 15 SW7s and SW9s, six Baldwin VO1000s, a single VO660, and four GE 44-tonners were added. By 1950, the diesel switcher fleet totaled 43 units.

For road service, 52 F-type units were purchased from EMD, along with 37 GP7s. The cab units were delivered between 1948 and 1951 and included 32 A-units and 20 Bs. Twenty one units were F3s, while the balance were F7s.

Continuing the dual-service mode set earlier by 4-8-2 and 4-8-4 steamers, the Fs alternated in both passenger and fast freight service from Atlanta to Nashville, and eventually to Memphis. The B-units contained steam generators for passenger service, while all units had steam and signal lines. Unlike the L&N, NC&StL opted for dynamic brakes on its Fs.

The 37 GP7s were delivered in 1950 and '51. The first six rode on switcher trucks instead of the usual EMD Blomberg trucks. The 25 units which followed were conventional GP7s, while the last five came with steam generators for passenger service and were painted blue and gray.

The first yard switchers wore black, but later NC paint diagrams called for oxide red with yellow lettering and striping for switchers and most of the GP7s.

All F type cab units, plus the last five dual-purpose Geeps wore an attractive blue and gray scheme with red heralds. NC&StL's 132-unit diesel fleet was absorbed into the L&N roster in August 1957. Most units remained in service and were renumbered by merely adding 1,000 to the older NC&StL numbers.

H. C. Hill/L&N Collection, U of L Archives

K2D heavy 4-6-2 535 was streamlined in 1947 for NC&StL's *City of Memphis* coach streamliner. The blue-gray Pacific got a quick bath at West Nashville during the train's midday layover in the Music City before returning to Memphis that afternoon.

J. Parker Lamb

NC&StL used its 37 GP7s on locals, branch lines and as helpers on Cumberland Mountain. Five Geeps, with boilers, also doubled on passenger when needed. In September 1959, two years after the L&N merger, two former NC Geeps, by then renumbered but still in original paint, headed out of Bruceton, Tenn., with the Union City Branch local freight.

To augment locomotive and rolling stock repair work done in Louisville, the L&N in 1890 opened a new shop facility at Albany, Ala., just south of Decatur. An 1890s view of the complex revealed principal shop buildings there as well as various cars being overhauled out of doors. During the early 1900s, L&N also maintained smaller shops at Birmimgham, Corbin, Etowah, Evansville and Paris, Tenn.

All 24 stalls of the South Louisville round-house were full, occupied mostly by Mikado-type freight power, in this June 1946 view. The bell tower of nearby Holy Name Church was visible in the background.

Wm. C. Tayse/L&N Collection, University of Louisville Archives

After 1905, L&N concentrated the bulk of heavy repairs as well as new construction at its South Louisville Shops, the campus occupying over 70 acres. Looking south, a 1974 aerial view showed, at bottom center, Shop 17 for diesel running repairs and locomotive servicing facilities, just to the right. Heavy repairs for locomotives were performed in long horizontal building center of photo, while freight car repairs and upgrading programs were concentrated in silver-roofed buildings, at upper left. Main line to Nashville cut diagonally across scene at top right.

LOUISVILLE & NASHVILLE

The Old Reliable

BLT 5 42

L&N was known for much of its history as "The Old Reliable."

Freight Car Potpourri

If a railroading Rip Van Winkle were to have started his extended snooze in, say 1940, upon awakening 20 years later, he would have been thunder-struck at all manner of innovations which had transpired in the intervening decades to forever change the rail scene he once knew. Especially would that have been true in the realm of motive power and rolling stock throughout the industry, and certainly on the L&N. This chapter explores by word and picture some of that dimension of change as it impacted L&N's freight car fleet and, most especially, as its fleet evolved from a basic "plain Jane" batch of cars and types to one of the most diversified freight fleets in the nation.

L&N's motivation in the Post World War II years was to match and tailor its freight cars to the specialized needs of its shippers. Editors Nancy Ford and Ed Myers of *Modern Railroads* made these observations about L&N equipment in a full-length feature on the L&N in the July 1967 issue of MR: "In tailoring its freight

fleet to meet customer needs, L&N took factors of rate and train service into account, but went further and engineered special loading and unloading conveniences into the cars, as well as devices for insuring greater safety for the lading." Concluded Ford and Myers, "The L&N has been a leader in promoting, purchasing and even building some of these specialized cars."

These pages will highlight some of L&N's more recent equipment acquisitions and its efforts at specialization. L&N's freight car fleet in 1963 totaled some 58,300 cars; of that number, some 33,000 were open-top hoppers, including over 8,000 of 70- and 100-ton capacity, most assigned to coal service. Box cars, ranging from 50- to 100-ton capacity, made up the next largest group of cars, or about 15,000 units. The remaining cars included high- and low-sided gondolas, covered hopper cars, wood chip hoppers, flats, bulkhead flats and several heavy duty multi-axle flats. Commercial car builders delivered most of the

L&N Collection, University of Louisville Archives

No. 8893, a 40-foot, 40-ton boxcar typified L&N's pre-World War II boxcar fleet. Built in 1920s, car had steel underframe, wood superstructure.

In the post-World War II years, L&N bought hundreds of 40-foot, 50-ton boxcars like No. 16626, a 1947 Mt. Vernon Car Manufacturing (Division of Pressed Steel Car Co.) product in series 15000-16799. Many were later upgraded.

new car orders, although the South Louisville Shops Car Department took on special orders as well as continuing to upgrade older car series.

The 40-foot, 50 ton boxcars, long "maids of all work" for the road, were joined by 70- and 100-ton cars, some with special interior equipment for loading and some with double doors; others were outfitted to carry specific commodities such as auto parts, appliances, grocery products and paper rolls. Singularly striking were the huge 86-foot long "high cube" auto-parts cars which entered service in the mid-1960s to handle light weight but bulky auto parts from parts manufacturers to assembly plants.

Also impressive in appearance and size were the big 100-ton covered hopper cars which L&N bought in large numbers beginning in the early 1960s to move bulk commodities, notably corn, grains, soybeans and other farmbelt products. The ACF-built cars, with their "inverted teardrop" cross section configurations, featured full-length trough loading hatches. Painted blue with yellow lettering and numerals, the cars were quickly dubbed "Big Blues."

L&N even achieved a color coding-of-sorts for much of its fleet. Blue not only denoted the above-described series of 100-ton covered hopper cars, but the color was applied generally to all boxcars of 70-ton or higher capacity, if the cars were equipped with damage-free ("DF") or interior load-protective devices. Orange helped identify 100-ton capacity open-top hoppers assigned to unit coal trains. Greens and tans made spotting certain other covered hopper cars, some in grain service, others assigned to moving diverse bulk commodities like cement and ores.

To match the new gray-yellow color scheme introduced by its second-generation diesel power in the early 1960s, L&N began painting its new steel cabooses in like colors. However, before the decade was out, South Louisville's paint shop was back at work, painting earlier cabooses and more recent additions to the fleet the traditional "caboose" red. Along with representative freight car types, cabooses and other non-revenue cars are more fully described in the photo section that follows.

L&N Collection, University of Louisville Archives

Shipper demands for high-capacity boxcars prompted L&N in early 1960s to convert several hundred older 40-foot, single-door cars into 50-foot, 50- and 70-ton cars with 16-foot double-doors. Mounted on trucks and dollies, old 1947 vintage car was spread apart so South Louisville Shops carmen could weld in new pre-assembled center sill section that increased its length, cubic capacity.

Other specialty car types in L&N's fleet were: giant 7,000 cubic foot woodchip hopper cars (open top); multi-wheeled heavy-duty flat cars for oversized boilers and vessels; low-sided 50- and 60-foot gondolas, augmented by high-sided 100-ton capacity gons with detachable covers; bulkhead flats, of 50-, 70- and 100-ton capacity, for palletized lumber, wallboard, brick and pipe; woodrack cars, to move pulpwood from rural cutting yards to paper mills; heavy duty flat cars with end-of-car pedestals and tie-downs to transport a half-dozen or more large trucks in stack™back fashion; and, modified flats with upright members to handle aircraft wings.

But, let the photos and their descriptions tell more!

L&N Collection, University of Louisville Archives

With new doors, side and roof sheets and load-protective or "DF" gear, "stretched" 99732 emerged from South Louisville's paint shop, resplendent in blue and yellow in fall 1962. For quick identification, L&N painted "DF" box cars in 'blue, with yellow lettering.

C. Norman Beasley/L&N Collection, University of Louisville Archives

L&N also equipped many of its boxcars with special cargo-cushioning devices, such as long-travel couplers, draft gear and underframes, interior belt rails and partitions. ACF-built in 1960 and so equipped, blue 50-ton 97857 and sisters (series 97855-99) served the paper industry

L&N Collection
University of Louisville Archives

Jumbo 100- ton, 60-foot 105000 and 49 sisters, turned out by Pullman-Standard in 1962, were designed for high value manufactured products. DF-equipped, car also had aluminum doors, roof.

L&N Collection, University of Louisville Archives

L&N's largest boxcars were group of 86-foot long, 10,000 cubic foot auto-parts cars designed to carry bulky parts like fenders, hoods to assembly plants in the south. Big cars had double doors, were painted blue with yellow lettering.

WM. C. Tayse/L&N Collection, University of Louisville Archives

Berwick Forge produced 80 high-roof 70- ton boxcars like 410185, above, in 1973. Assigned to GE's Appliance Park, Louisville, 410185 and several sisters boasted 13-foot interior roof clearance, 10-foot doors, were painted in new "Family Lines" color scheme of black with yellow lettering, numerals

L&N Collection, University of Louisville Archives
Above: To transport aircraft wings produced at Lockheed-Georgia near Marietta and several other plants, L&N in 1960s designed and built small fleet of cars. No. 24953, shown at Lockheed in 1969, utilized well-shaped bottom, vertical deck bracing to handle wings, tail sections for L1011's, other big planes then being assembled by Lockheed.

Charles B. Castner/L&N Collection, University of Louisville Archives
Left: In 1959, L&N converted group of 50-ton, 56-foot flat cars (vintage 1947, by Greenville Car Co.)into bulkhead flats. No. 24962 (series 24957-89) was loaded with poles at the T. R. Miller Mill Co., in Brewton, AL., in 1965.

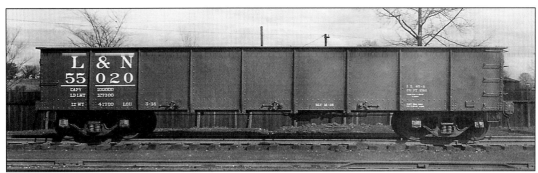

L&N Collection, University of Louisville Archives

L&N No. 55020, a 40-foot, 50-ton gon built in 1925 by Pressed Steel Car Co., Pittsburgh, was at South Louisville in 1938 after shopping. Car was in series, 54000-56499, many being used in Kentucky coal fields.

L&N Collection, University of Louisville Archives

Standard 50-ton, two-pocket opentop hoppers like 181606 were mainstays of L&N's hopper fleet from 1920s through 1950s and advent of larger capacity cars. Built in 1923, the 181606 got a new facelift (and the "Old Reliable" slogan) at South Louisville Shops in 1951. Carbody paint scheme was red, with white lettering and numerals.

C. Norman Beasley/L&N Collection, University of Louisville Archives

During early 1960s, many old 50-ton opentop hoppers like 119507 (in series 115000-119999) were upgraded with higher side and end sheets at South Louisville Shops.

Pullman-Standard/L&N Collection, University of Louisville Archives

In late 1957, L&N began buying Pullman-Standard's popular PS-3 three-pocket 70-ton hopper car for coal service, and P-S's Bessemer, AL., plant assembled 2,000 PS-3's for the road during 1957-8. Later 1959 order produced another batch,including 150081, which was Pullman-Standard's l0,000th PS-3.

Wm. C. Tayse/L&N Collection, University of Louisville Archives
Still bigger hoppers joined the fleet in mid-1960s, as L&N launched more fast-load unit coal trains. Gleaming in orange paint, big 100-ton bottom-dump 190231 and sisters rolled from South Louisville's paint shop in late December 1963. Shops designed and built 50- car series, each with stainless steel slope sheets, motor-activated unloading doors.

Big car order of late 1969-70 included 875 80-ton, three pocket red opentop hoppers like 182699, from Bethlehem Steel Company; Pullman-Standard also delivered 1,200 similar 80-tonners in same acquisition, most for coal fields.

Rail industry's largest woodchip hopper 31002, second of 50-car series built by Ortner Freight Car Co., dwarfed rebuilt 50-tonner 84382 in display at Union Station in fall 1963. With six discharge gates, giant 31002 offered 7,000 cubic feet versus 2,200 for smaller 84382. High cube capacity also enabled L&N to offer incentive rates to paper mills, pulp yards.

Pullman-Standard designed and built experimental "Side-Gate 100 XHC" in 1967. With lever-operated side discharge panels, 199999 was intended for unit coal train use but could be modified for bulk commodities. L&N tested but never had car duplicated.

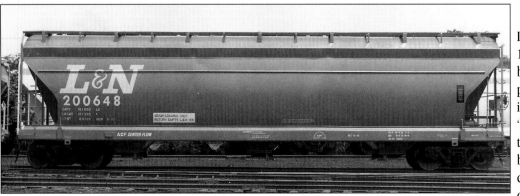

L&N liked ACF's big "center flow" 100-ton covered hoppers so well, it bought hundreds during 1960s, painted them blue with yellow lettering. Cars (which employees called "Big Blues") featured topside trough hatches for faster grain and bulk commodity loadings, three discharge gates; 200648 was in 1970 order of 100 units.

Wm. C. Tayse/L&N Collection,
University of Louisville Archives

Short-lived (1983-86) Seaboard System brought together SCL, L&N, Clinchfield and the Georgia/West Point roads under "two S" red-yellow logo and color scheme. At Rice Yard in Waycross, GA., in 1983, dark gray GP16 "Tampa Rebuilds" paused beneath yard hump, string of freight equipment in new SBD paint.

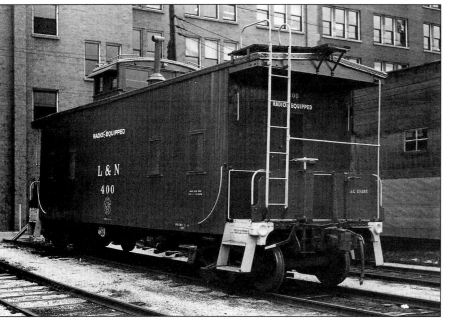

C. Norman Beasley/L&N Collection,
University of Louisville Archives

During late 1940s and 1950s, South Louisville converted a hundred or more 40-ton, 40-foot wood boxcars into road and transfer cabooses. Radio-equipped cab 400, spotted at the General Office Building in January 1954, was painted red with yellow steps, grab irons and ladders. Logo, numerals were white. Transfer cabs were rebuilt without cupolas.

Ron Flanary Collection

Forty-foot 552 typified hundreds of wooden cabooses L&N rostered before and just after World War II, many built at South Louisville Shops. Old 552, from Louisville in 1921, somehow survived to 1969 where, in March, she was found at Cowan, TN. Traditional color- red with white lettering, yellow steps and grab irons

Wm. C. Tayse/L&N Collection, University of Louisville Archives

To replace aging fleet of wood cabooses, South Louisville Shops beginning in 1963 designed and assembled several hundred steel bay-window cabs; 1020, on ready tracks at South Louisville in February 1964, was from first order of 100, was painted gray with red letters, yellow steps and trim.

Ron Flanary

South Louisville-built cab 1148 brought up rear of CV Division fast freight No.65 at Loyall, Ky., in July 1965. Later in decade, L&N repainted all cabs bright red with yellow lettering, also built series with longer car bodies.

Epilogue

For former employees, friends, fans and others with an affection for railroads like the L&N, it's difficult to "close the books," so to speak, or to neatly wrap up and file away what, in L&N's case, amounted to well over a century and a quarter of effort, struggle and achievement. What's more, one is hard put to have sketched a different scenario for the road's survival.

The loss of the L&N as a corporate entity has not necessarily meant the demise of a once great rail property. To the contrary, CSX Transportation and its corporate parent have built on strengths and traditions formed by past legions of L&N, C&EI, Monon, NC&StL and TC folk; CSXT has also expanded and refined those physical properties, tying them together to stimulate further growth. Strong and well managed, the surviving company has put in place a sound organization, has achieved decent returns for its owners and stockholders, and has pushed its sphere of service and influence far beyond continental geographic limits envisioned by its predecessors. With a new century just ahead, there is the real prospect of a railroad renaissance and, indeed,

Al Chione Collection

Baldwin-built M-1 No. 1953 worked hard across the Red River bridge with a Ravenna-DeCoursey coal train in 1955. "Big Emma" 2-8-4's handled tonnage trains all the way, except for an uphill segment from Ravenna north to Winchester (Patio), Ky., which required a second M-1 pushing behind the caboose.

It's the late 1950s, and we're aboard *Boston Club*, a tavern-lounge built in 1946 by American Car & Foundry for the Cincinnati-New Orleans *Humming Bird*. The car was originally named *Churchill Downs*, which explains the thoroughbred horse motif on the glass partition.

a bright future for these, the railroads of our affection.

Happily, some of the lore and tradition of the L&N live on. That's due in no little part to efforts of many friends and fans who, formally and informally, have sought to save something of what might be called the "essence" of the L&N. On the formal side, several organizations should be recognized for their preservation work.

The L&N Historical Society, organized in 1982, has grown to count at this writing over 1,000 members scattered from coast to coast as well as in several overseas countries. Its members help preserve the L&N "story" through modeling projects, advocacy and protection of prototype equipment, publishing magazines and newsletters and republishing some former company documents. The NC&StL has also

received its due from the L&NHS, while two similar organizations, the C&EI Historical Society (based in Crestview, Ill.) and the Monon Historical & Technical Society (in Lafayette, Ind.) have done much to build their own collections of artifacts and materials pertaining to those former railroads.

The Kentucky Railway Museum had its birth in Louisville in 1957 and located soon after on riverfront property served by an L&N spur. Centerpiece of KRM's equipment holdings then (as well as now) was former L&N steam locomotive, No. 152, a Rogers 1905 light Pacific type, which KRMers restored to operation in 1985. Today, the Museum operates from New Haven, in rural Nelson County, Ky., on some 20 miles of abandoned Lebanon Branch trackage it acquired from CSX

On NC&StL trackage between Cartersville and Atlanta, Ga., a Knoxville & Atlanta Division fast freight rolled out of a cut in 1953. The L&N south of Knoxville was an early convert to diesel power, with Alcos like these FA/FB2 units handling the through trains.

Transportation in 1990.

Complementing No. 152 is former Monon BL2 diesel No. 32 and a fine roster of vintage rolling stock, including coaches, Pullmans and head-end cars of definitive L&N and NC&StL lineage. In mid-summer 1995, the Museum opened a new station building to house and display its large collection of smaller artifacts; depot space is also allocated for a ticket office and gift shop. The structure replicates the former brick station that once served L&N in New Haven.

The University of Louisville Archives at Ekstrom Library on the Belknap campus preserves a select collection of L&N corporate records donated to it when the Louisville General Office Building was closed in 1988 and last departments relocated elsewhere. The collection includes papers of several of L&N's chairmen and presidents, a complete run of company employee magazines (1925-1974), many years of public timetables, also a file of promotional photographs and negatives produced over the decades by the L&N public relations department staff and other photographers.

Several other organizations should be mentioned for their efforts to protect something of the L&N: the Bluegrass Railroad Museum, in Versailles, Ky., near Lexington; The Tennessee Valley Railroad in Chattanooga; and the West Florida Railroad Museum, in Milton, Fla. The last-named group has masterfully restored L&N's former wood frame depot there and has surrounded the building with rolling stock and other paraphernalia of L&N origins. Other museums and organizations, unknown to the authors, should be commended, regardless, for

Restored to full operating condition, the historic engine "General" and Combine 665 were spotted on L&N's Beargrass Spur in Louisville for publicity shots in March 1962. They were shortly to embark on a two-year tour for Civil War Centennial commemorative events.

their work and interest in saving a bit of the L&N and its "family of railroads" in their several collections.

The former NC&StL was often referred to as "Grandpa's Road," for the reason that generations of men and women followed their parents and grandparents into the service of that company. Reunions of the "Old Guard," as senior employees and retirees came to be known, were and continue to be held regularly across that system. The larger L&N also shared like familial employment patterns, with younger generations succeeding their parents and grandparents "on the railroad." Continuing today, groups of former and retired employees, from L&N ranks as well as those of

the Monon and NC&StL, gather periodically for formal reunions or more informal sessions at diverse locations. They too are helping preserve a legacy from the past.

Much has been written over the decades about the L&N, and as the bibliography will attest, the scope of that body of literature can also testify to the Old Reliable's life and times, its successes and achievements as well as times when it stubbed its corporate toe, so to speak. We like especially what the editors of RAILWAY AGE had to say, as they concluded coverage of the L&N in their December 28, 1970 issue:

"On occasion, the frankest assessment of a railroad and of a management can come from

J. B. Fravert Photo

M-1 1966 got a shot of sand at DeCoursey Roundhouse in April 1956. The heavily weathered appearance of the 2-8-4 was typical for L&N freight-service power, although at that late date for steam, the engines looked even shabbier.

the outside— from other railroaders who work with and/or compete with the people they are assessing. On this score, L&N comes off with high marks, today and for tomorrow. Two long-time L&N watchers sum up L&N this way: 'They are unflappable. They may not make much notice about it—but that's a good railroad!'"

The late *Trains* editor David P. Morgan was a great fan and friend of the L&N, and his unabashed enthusiasm for the line showed up in issue after issue of his publication. Son of a Presbyterian Minister, a Georgian by birth and a Wisconsin resident for much of his adult life, Morgan might be suspect for his loyalty to the L&N. But that affection was valid; his early exposure to the road resulted from a seven- or eight-year period in the mid 1930s and early 1940s, during which time his father pastored

the Crescent Hill Presbyterian Church, in Louisville's suburban east end. Several L&N families were members of the Reverend Dr. Morgan's congregation.

The manse the Morgans occupied during their Kentucky tenure sat just a block north of L&N's double-tracked Short Line main to Cincinnati and Eastern Kentucky. Yes, Louisville was served by other railroads, among them Eastern giants Pennsy and New York Central. But, it was L&N—its trains and locomotives, its people and its uniquely "home town" way of operating and doing business— that so captivated and charmed young David Morgan. He was never to forget Old Reliable or its trains.

Editor Morgan's full length feature story, "This is Louisville & Nashville" appeared in March 1955 *Trains,* and it sketched an L&N on

L-1 4-8-2 409, at South Louisville Roundhouse about 1950, displayed L&N's livery for passenger steam power: Silver trim on cylinder heads and running boards; red number plate and herald (under cab window); black boiler jacket and tender; yellow lettering and numerals

the eve of dieselization. In the estimation of these writers, that story must stand as one of the best essays about the L&N. In searching for an elusive essence of his favorite railroad, Morgan wrote:

"L&N is, in a mouthful, a curious mixture of conservatism, Southern sympathies, humility, and a healthy respect for the honest buck. On its record....that's a successful if unspectacular way to run a railroad. But for all of its obscurity—and it is perhaps America's least-known major railroad—L&N can operate with the best of them... . "

Morgan concluded: "So you attempt to pin down a 4,737-mile railroad with a typewriter, trying to catch in its keys something of the essential about L&N's 62,800 freight cars, Radnor yard and 1,205 miles of C.T.C. and $120,000 worth of Bendix and Motorola radio equipment—about this railroad now worth almost $755 million and about what its 23,000 men and women do with it. You try to set forth its principles of policy, especially those which give meaning to the slogan 'Old

Reliable,' and you seek to explain how (L&N) has saved money and made money so that in hard times and good it can continue to render a public service, pay decent wages regularly, and furnish a safe investment for even a widow's pennies."

Much later, in the May 1976 TRAINS, Morgan was to again write about the L&N, for that issue a lovely remembrance of his growing-up years at trackside in Louisville. As a title, he used the first verse of the old Irish ballad, *Mother Machree*. In Morgan's hand, it became:

"There's a spot in my heart
which no other railroad may own,
There's a depth in my soul
never sounded or known,
There's a place in my memory,
my life, that you fill,
No other can take it, none ever will."

To which we can only add, Amen, brothers and sisters, Amen!

L&N Historical Society Collection

Above: L&N's beautiful blue and cream paint scheme was introduced in 1942 by its first 16 road diesels. Designed by Electro-Motive's styling department, the original livery was displayed by E6 753 at Louisville in 1953. To the left, units 752 and 781 are ready to head north to Cincinnati with train 4, the *Azalean*.

Al Chione Collection

Below: Train 94, the northbound *Dixie Flyer*, rolled across the Etowah River near Cartersville, Ga., on February 12, 1958. Although this scene was made six months after the L&N-NC&StL merger , a pair of F-units in the former NC's familiar blue-gray scheme handled the head-end-heavy train.

L&N Historical Society Collection

An aerial view of the sprawling South Louisville Shops complex shows just how large the plant really was. "Shop One" (erecting shop for heavy locomotive repairs) extended from left to right near the center of this view. The long metal-roofed building on the left housed "Shops 13-14" for freight car repairs. At lower left was "Shop 17," the running repair facility for diesels. At the bottom was the locomotive servicing area (grassy area was site of the old steam roundhouse). The mainline to Nashville ran along the right side of the photo, with South Louisville Yard at top right. This view, from 1974, looked southward.

L&N Historical Society Collection

In March 1974, the 42-bay erecting shop at South Louisville held an unusual mix of diesel power under repair. From the foreground back is a GE U25C, an Alco C628, SW7 No. 2226, GP9 543 (ex-C&EI), another Geep, C630 1430, an SD40, plus several other units.

Bright blue 70-ton boxcar 100001 was built by American Car & Foundry in 1962. These cars became familiar sights all over the L&N system, as more freight began to move in "DF" (damage free-equipped) cars like #100001.

After absorbing NC&StL in 1957, L&N adopted its affiliate's "Dixie Line" slogan and began substituting it in place of "Old Reliable" on rolling stock. ACF-built 50-ton boxcar 97892, outshopped in 1960, was one of the earlier cars equipped with an impact reducing hydra-cushion underframe.

L&N designed and built a fleet of rapid-dump 100-ton open top hoppers in 1964-65 for unit trains serving the Tennessee Valley Authority. These movements originated on the Eastern Kentucky Subdivision and handled coal to TVA's Bull Run Steam Plant, near Oak Ridge, Tenn. A test shipment was being unloaded at Bull Run in 1965.

T. M. Taylor/L&N Historical Society Collection

Above: On July 26, 1962, a southbound "Automobile Special" rounded a curved at Wauhatchie near Chattanooga, with Raccoon Mountain in the background. The December 1962 TRAINS Magazine featured L&N's movement of automotive traffic by tracing a new Ford and its rail trip from Louisville to Atlanta.

Tom Smart Photo/Ron Flanary Collection

Lower Right: New SDP35 No. 1703, at DeCoursey Yard in December 1965, was one of four such units acquired by the L&N that year to replace aging E-units. Although designed for both freight and passenger use, the four ended up hauling only tonnage during their service lives.

Second generation L&N power was grouped at DeCoursey Yard, Ky., for this impressive lineup in 1964. From left to right are three Alco C628's, a pair of GE U25B's, two EMD GP30's, and single "four aces" EMD GP35 no. 1111. The scene appeared on the cover of the December 1964 *L&N Magazine*.

A sunny November morning in 1964 brightened the yellow nose of E6 774 leading No. 98, the northbound *Pan-American*, at Birmingham. L&N had modified the engine only slightly since its 1942 delivery by adding F-style number boards, solid side panels plus a few more hand rails.

L&N's first road-switcher units from EMD were GP7's, built in 1952. Shortly after delivery, No. 417, in black and cream livery, paused between chores at Lebanon Junction, Ky. in early 1953.

Outshopped by Baldwin in April 1944, VO1000 No. 2207 was one of the earlier diesel yard switchers on L&N's roster. The rugged unit was at work at Louisville's Union Station in 1953.

C. Norman Beasley/L&N Historical Society Collection

Above: L&N's first "named" freight train was the Cincinnati-New Orleans *Silver Bullet*. The train, headed by a shiny foursome of F-units, was pictured at South Louisville Yard in 1953 before resuming its nocturnal dash southward.

L&N Collection/UofL Archives

Left: Two-way radio communications in the rail industry had entered the era of minaturazation when this photo was made. A switchman at Louisville's Strawberry yard modeled an early "chest pack" radio in 1964.

W. Terrell Dickey/Charles B. Castner Collection

Veteran Short Line Conductor Henry Edmundson, right, and Engineer Al Lacher checked train orders at Union Station, Louisville, before taking the *Azalean* north to Cincinnati in September 1963.

Bibliography

Books:

Castner, Charles B., Jr.; *Nashville, Chattanooga & St. Louis Railway-Dixie Line*; Carstens Publications, Newton, N.J., 1995;

Clark, Thomas A.; *The Beginning Of The L&N; Development Of The Louisville & Nashville R.R. And Its Memphis Branch From 1836 To 1860*; Standard Publishing Co., Louisville, Ky., 1933;

Dolzall, Gary W. & Stephen F.; *Monon, The Hoosier Line*; Interurban Press, Trans-Angelo Books, Glendale, Cal., 1987;

Drury, George; *Historical Guide To North American Railroads*; Kalmbach Books, Kalmbach Publishing Co., Milwaukee, Wis., 1985;

Flanary, Ronald C.(with Oroszi & McKee); *The L&N In The Appalachians*; Old Line Graphics, Silver Spring, Md., 1990;

Herr, Kincaid; *Louisville & Nashville Railroad, 1850-1959*; 3rd Edition, Published by the railroad, Louisville, Ky., 1959;

Hilton, George W.; *Monon Route*; Howell-North Books, Berkeley, Cal., 1978;

Kerr, Joseph G.; *Historical Development Of The Louisville & Nashville Railroad System*; published by the railroad; printed by Westerfield-Bonte Co., Louisville, Ky., 1926;

Key, R. Lyle; *Midwest-Florida Sunliners*; RPC Publications, Godfrey, IL., 1979;

Klein, Maury; *History Of The Louisville & Nashville Railroad*; The MacMillan Co., New York, 1972; and *Unfinished Business: Railroads In American Life*; University Press of New England, London, N.H., 1994;

Prince, Richard E.; *Louisville & Nashville Steam Locomotives, Revised Edition, 1968, and Nashville, Chattanooga & St. Louis History & Steam Locomotives*; 1967, both published by the author, Green River, Wy.;

Stover, John F.; *Railroads Of The South*; Chapel Hill, University of North Carolina Press, 1955;

Sulzer, Elmer G.; *Ghost Railroads Of Kentucky*; Vane A. Jones, Co., Indianapolis, Ind., 1967;

Tilford, John E.; *L&N, Its First 100 Years* (Reprint of Address), published by Newcomen Society of North America, 1951;

Official Railroad Documents and Publications (L&N, NC&StL):

Annual Reports to Stockholders (CSX Corp., L&N and SCL Industries), 1940-1994;

Directory of Coal Mines On The L&N; Issued by Coal Department, Louisville, Ky., 1965;

Division by Division, The L&N Today; Public Relations & Advertising Department, Louisville, Ky., 1966;

Pictorial History Of The L&N; Public Relations & Advertising Dept., Louisville, Ky., 1972

L&N, Private Builder & Public Servant-Years of Noteworthy Achievement (with Statistical Tables); Public Relations & Advertising Department, Louisville, Ky., 1954;

L&N Railroad Under The Leadership of John E. Tilford; Public Relations & Advertising Department, Louisville, Ky., 1959;

Division line profiles; equipment, motive power data books, diagrams and summaries; miscellaneous promotional booklets and pamphlets; public and operating timetables; station lists;

Family Lines, published by Corporate Communications Department, Louisville, Ky., 1974-1981;

L&N Magazine, published by Advertising & Publications, Public Relations Departments, Louisville, Ky., 1925-1974;

L&N Historical Society Collection

Employees leave the Broadway entrance of L&N's General Office Building in downtown Louisville in 1960. First wing of 11-story building opened in 1907, and second wing was added in 1930. Union Station was just a block away.

Periodicals and other Publications:

Dixie Line, "Toto, L&N's First Decade of Piggyback Service," Parts 1 & 2, By Lee Gordon, L&N Historical Society, August & October 1993;

Modern Railroads, "The Modern L&N, Leader in High Capacity Railroading," by Nancy Ford and Edw. T. Myers; July 1967;

Railroad Magazine, "A Century of Steam on the L&N," by Charles B. Castner, Jr., December 1964;

Railway Age, "L&N — Looking Toward Growth in '70s," December 28, 1970; and "Great Railroads; Family Lines Gets Its Act Together;" by Frank Malone, September 10, 1979;

Trains; "This is Louisville & Nashville," by David P. Morgan, March 1955; "Big Emma," by Charles B. Castner, Jr., December 1972; and "Olden Times on Old Reliable," by David P. Morgan, May 1976.

L&N Historical Society Collection

L&N wooden caboose 158 was part of equipment display at Louisville in 1956. "Traditional" caboose paint scheme included red carbody, yellow steps, grabirons and ladders, and white lettering and numerals.